Meeting Christ in Teens
Startling Moments of Grace

John Rosengren

Saint Mary's Press, Winona, Minnesota

For my parents, who blessed me with their faith.

The grace that has come my way has provided countless occasions for gratitude. Here's a limited expression of thanks.

My parents raised me well. They instilled my faith. They loved me without giving up. They taught me to say please and thank you. What goes around comes around. Thank you, Mom and Dad.

Thank you, Roger Mahn, for modeling the gift of believing in teenagers.

Thank you, Bob Zyskowski, for believing my initial idea deserved space in your fine newspaper.

Thank you, Archbishop Harry Flynn, for your generous and gentle support.

Thank you, Leif Kehrwald, for believing these columns could become a book.

Thank you to all the students who served as my teacher and revealed God's grace to me.

Thank you, God, for everything.

The publishing team included Leif Kehrwald, development editor; Cären Yang, art director; Cindi Ramm, design director; Alan S. Hanson, pre-press specialist; manufactured by the production services department of Saint Mary's Press.

Produced with the assistance of D&G Limited, LLC. Project staff included: Janette Lynn, copy editor; D&G Limited, LLC, production editor and typesetter; Tina Williams, cover designer.

The acknowledgments continue on page 119.

 Genuine recycled paper with 10% post consumer waste. Printed with soy-based ink.

Copyright © 2002 by John Rosengren. All rights reserved. No part of this book may be reproduced by any means without the written permission of the publisher.

Printed in the United States of America
Printing: 9 8 7 6 5 4 3 2 1
Year: 2010 09 08 07 06 05 04 03 02

Library of Congress Cataloging-in-Publication Data

Rosengren, John.
   Meeting Christ in teens : startling moments of grace / John Rosengren.
      p. cm.
   Includes bibliographical references.
   ISBN 0-88489-739-7 (alk. paper)
     1. Teenagers—Religious life. I. Title.
BV4447.R665 2002
248.8'3—dc21

2002008630

Contents

Introduction	4
Chapter 1 When We Practice Compassion	8
Chapter 2 When We Speak Up	21
Chapter 3 When We Look for It	34
Chapter 4 When We Let It	50
Chapter 5 When We See Beyond Stereotypes	63
Chapter 6 When We Serve	76
Chapter 7 When We Are Grateful	89
Chapter 8 When We Enter into Life's Mysteries	100
Conclusion	117

Introduction

Teenagers have confounded adults for centuries. As early as Aristotle, the older generation complained about the younger generation's limitations and excesses. That hasn't changed. These days, teens sling slang we can't understand. They wear clothes we wouldn't. And on and on to the point that the teenager label has become laden with negative connotations. Yet throughout eleven years as a teacher and counselor in public and Catholic high schools, many of those years spent at Saint Thomas Academy in Mendota Heights, Minnesota, I encountered teenagers who regularly defied that stereotype.

Daily, I pleasantly and refreshingly discovered the goodness and wisdom of students. I learned that we adults have as many lessons to learn from young people as we aspire to bestow upon them. My students taught me humor, gratitude, integrity, sportsmanship, humility, compassion, desire, courage, caring, patience—and so much more. They taught me to see the face of God spotted with acne.

Those lessons were moments of grace. God became present to me through them. In my daily interactions with those teenagers, I encountered Christ.

That's what these columns are about. Written over a period of three years and first published in *The Catholic Spirit* (the newspaper of the diocese of Saint Paul–Minneapolis, where I live), each column illustrates a moment of grace—God's love, presence, beauty, or goodness—as revealed in daily life.

Once we start seeing Christ in teenagers and becoming aware of God's presence and grace in our interactions with them, we discover the same in other situations. These reflections focus mainly on moments with students but also venture into a pottery class, a friend's disease, and traffic jams, among other places. There's no limit to where we'll meet God's grace, but with each column, I try to apply that grace to our connections with teenagers.

During the column's run from 1996 to 1999, hardly a day went by that I did not hear from readers. They called, wrote letters, approached me in restaurants—always to let me know that what they'd read had struck a chord. I realized that people, wearied by the media bombardment of bad news—and the centuries-old teenager stereotype—want to read uplifting thoughts on how God's presence is revealed, especially through young people.

My Own Youth

My own adolescent struggles have given me a special sensitivity toward teenagers.

I grew up in a stable household founded upon my parents' faith, but I developed an early love affair with alcohol and marijuana. At fifteen, I was already worried about my drug use. Friends drank to drink; I drank to get drunk. They liked smoking pot; I loved it. That worried me.

I figured I'd transfer to a Catholic high school, clean up my act, and play varsity hockey. I loved hockey as much as anything.

The Catholic school was smaller, my chances of making the team were better. I quit smoking dope and quit drinking. I trained. When tryouts arrived, I was in good shape. I prayed that I would make the team. To that point, my faith had been strong. Raised in a Catholic family, I had often felt close to God. I'd strayed some during my drinking and drugging but still believed. I wanted to make the hockey team, and I believed God could help me.

I got cut. I felt betrayed. I'd done my part; God hadn't done His. In my hurt, I rationalized that I didn't need a god who didn't answer my prayers. I resumed smoking and drinking heavily. I transferred back to the local public high school. I spent every day of spring trimester my junior year stoned. I never played varsity hockey.

I got caught, over and over. Coming home drunk, smoking pot, stealing booze, breaking curfew, and so on. I lied to my parents, my coaches, my teachers. I felt guilty, ashamed, worthless. I got high. Over and over—the cycle repeated itself.

Autumn of my senior year, I got busted at a party, drunk and stoned. After listening to my slurred insults, the cop who took me downtown was kind enough not to kick my teeth in but to drop me off safely at detox. My parents were brave enough not to bail me out but to let me suffer the consequences of my actions, which included four days shuffling about in paper slippers and thin pajamas behind locked doors. The counselors at the treatment center where I wound up were patient enough not to give up on me but to teach me the paradox of surrendering to gain freedom. Through their help—and the grace of God—I got sober.

At seventeen, I had to start over. I had been a popular partier, a cocky kid with a quick wit and smart mouth. That had all been a shtick to cover up the pain and confusion and loneliness of adolescence. Without dope, I felt raw, vulnerable, and exposed. Who was I? What would I be?

Thank God for English teachers. Roger Mahn, my journalism teacher during my senior year, spotted what he deemed talent in the sports columns I scratched out for the student newspaper. He took a personal interest in me. During an independent study with him that year, the conversation during our one-on-one sessions was more likely to turn toward growing as a person than revising a lead paragraph. That's the way he was with all the students: Encouraging them to risk being themselves. He cared about us as people first, and we could tell.

For me, it worked. Roger helped me stay sober my senior year. He kindled an interest in writing. And he inspired me to teach. My parents had instilled a faith in me that Roger and others on the path of recovery restored. I am grateful for all of those along the way who have showered me with God's grace.

Now, when I see the fright in a young person's eyes or hear the struggles they're facing, I remember what it was like to walk in their shoes and have someone reach out to me. I want to do the same for them. I want to pass on the grace that I've been so freely given. That's allowed me to see God's grace at work from both sides.

As I reread these columns, I reminisced about students who are no longer a part of my daily life and appreciated them all over again. I'm grateful for the gifts they shared so generously with me. This book is my thank-you to them. I pass their stories along so that you, too, may appreciate their gifts—and those of the teens who are part of your lives.

Perhaps these columns will inspire you to seek the goodness in teens. Perhaps they will make you more aware of God's presence and grace active in your daily life. Perhaps they will spark discussion with your teenagers. My wish is that through God's grace they will lead you ultimately to encounter Christ.

Chapter 1
When We Practice Compassion

Introduction

Grace happens when we practice compassion—setting aside our own notions to see things from another's point of view, entering into their experience, knowing their suffering. That's compassion. It's an act of love. A gift of grace.

Compassion lets us remember that teenagers are a work in progress. That they're still learning what might seem second nature to us. That they're struggling where we, as adults, might sail smoothly.

The act of compassion shows respect and gains respect. That respect is necessary as a foundation of intimacy with the teenagers—and others—we care about. Respect lets us walk side by side with another.

To approach others with compassion, we set aside our expectations of who we want them to be. We approach them not with a desire to dominate but with the willingness to meet them at their level. We view them with God's eyes.

Compassion requires that we open our eyes and ears to see and hear the insecurities and sufferings that are otherwise invisible and silent. It requires that we open our hearts to others so that they'll open theirs to us.

Compassion is not spoken; it is acted. It is something we model, something we teach. It is an act that enables us to learn more than we might ever imagine possible from our younger teachers as they open up to us.

When we practice compassion, God's presence is revealed in our relationships.

grace

Take a Walk in Another's Moccasins

Growing up, I had a prayer hanging on my bulletin board: "Grant that I may not criticize my neighbor until I've walked a mile in his moccasins."

Often, that walk is taken with the ears. To listen to another's story is to learn what it is like to walk in that person's moccasins.

One day, several years ago, when I used to facilitate student support groups, the group's discussion drove home the message of that prayer. Alex, a vivacious and charming young man, came to group very upset. He'd been standing in the lunch line, wearing his new, black leather, Chicago Bulls cap that he was quite proud of, when a casual friend standing behind him said, "You're not going to turn nigger on us now, are you?"

Alex, a light-skinned African-American who was popular with the "in" crowd, was hurt that a white student would criticize him for what she perceived to be his identification with his race. She seemed to expect him to act "white"; that she would reject him for being who he was hurt him.

After Alex finished telling us what had happened to him, David spoke up. He talked about how he felt when kids would ask him, "Do you want to go fly a *kike?*" And how he felt when kids would kick pennies at him, expecting him to pick them up. And when kids in the cafeteria would ask him if his lunch was kosher.

Then Sally spoke up. She talked about how she felt when the male jocks in the commons put down her sport, saying volleyball was for sissies. And how she felt when teachers wouldn't call on her in math class. And about the hurtful reputations her female friends got for doing things with guys that seemed to boost the guys' reputations.

I just sat and listened. I'd had no idea that they experienced this sort of prejudice daily. But then, I wasn't black, Jewish, nor female, so I hadn't lived what they had. By telling me their stories, they let me in; they allowed me to walk in their moccasins.

As I listened, I learned the meaning of that prayer. Sometimes I presume to know what it's like for another, but that day those kids taught me that I don't have a clue what another's experiencing until I see life from his or her perspective.

I tell my students the story of that day's group when I hear them being critical of another for being different or when they seem to show no understanding of the ridicule and abuse some suffer in our society simply for being different. I tell them the message of that prayer, which is really about empathy. I ask them to place compassion before criticism.

· *grace* ·

Throwing Pots Is a Lot Like Raising Teens

Lately, as a student in an evening pottery class, I've been seeing things from the other side. I've learned a lot about teaching from this perspective.

The instructor makes throwing pots look so easy. She plops a lump of clay on the wheel, smoothly centers it, stretches the clay open, slides her hands along the sides—all in graceful motions—and she's got a pot. I splat my lump on the wheel, struggle to center it, watch the clay wobble uncertainly—push, pull, and prod—only to crush beneath my hands what was starting to look like a pot.

My struggles frustrate me. The instructor tells me to relax. Easy for her to say, I think, because this is easy for her to do. I forget that she's had years of training and practice that I haven't.

Here's the first lesson I've learned: What's easy for or obvious to us as adults might be something teenagers struggle with for the first time. Our experiences as students can teach us empathy and compassion by helping us to remember what it's like on the other side.

One night, I almost didn't go to class. I had grown tired of failure. But, not wanting to quit, I went. That night, something happened: The clay felt better in my hands; I made a pot. I mean a real pot, one that I'll be able to use and be proud to keep. The instructor told me the past efforts hadn't been failures, they'd simply been part of the process leading me to this one. (She's good, this instructor.) Lesson number two: Trust the process.

I'd made a pot with my own hands. I told everyone about that pot. (I'm telling you now.) I was so excited about it. I hadn't thought I could do it. Now, that pot's not going to be shown in any gallery nor sold for any sum, but it's valuable to me because it's mine. I made it. Lesson three: What might seem like small steps in others' eyes can be huge successes for an individual, especially for one who has struggled. Learning, maturing, and success are relative.

Throwing pots is a lot like raising teenagers. Sometimes, when we find ourselves fighting the clay and feeling hopeless, it might help to remember that we're still beginners, that everything is part of the process, and that our small successes are worth celebrating. That night that I made the pot, I felt "one" with the clay; it was shaping me as much as I was shaping it. That, too, might be helpful to remember.

· grace ·

They're Still Kids, Even the Big Ones

The other day, before we began our review for a test, I delivered my standard joke that copies of the test would go on sale after school, completed copies selling for fifty bucks, blanks for twenty. Several minutes into the review, one of the students raised his hand and said a bit sheepishly, "Are you really selling tests after school, because I don't want to be the only one to show up and feel stupid." The laughter from the other kids let him know he wouldn't have to wait until 2:40 for that.

It reminded me how vulnerable kids can be.

Thing is, they don't want you to know. They'll try to keep it from you. They'll laugh when they're hurt. They'll brush off attempts to talk. They'll tell you they don't care. They do their best to hide what they're feeling.

When we look at them and see the emerging adult in their bodies and faces, it's sometimes easy to fall for their defenses and go along with their facade that what we just said didn't hurt them. Or that they're not angry about the way a friend snubbed them. Or that they aren't scared about the upcoming exams.

It helps to remember the child inside. That's where they're vulnerable. Every now and then, they'll let us glimpse that child. When they show us the fear in their eyes, or they blush, or they're so broken they cry. Those moments jog the memory; they remind us of the tenderness within.

Problem is, I forget. Recently, I teased a student whom I've known for three years about something that I thought he'd take in stride. I was trying to use humor to make a point. His sarcastic response let me know I'd hurt him. I'd forgotten his vulnerability.

I'm still learning. Seems I forget this as often as I can remember. When I remember, though, I'm all right, because then I'm mindful of their vulnerability, and I can be gentle.

• *grace* •

Exposing the Politics of Humor

The talk turned to oppression. It happens every spring when the seniors do their comedy unit. A student told a joke that put down women. On the continuum of offensiveness, this particular joke fell toward the mild side, but it crossed the line with the negative stereotype the punch line reinforced.

One of the criteria for the students' jokes is that they not be offensive; the students are asked to stay on this side of the line between what's appropriate and what's not. Part of the learning process requires them to find where that line is. As with other behaviors, sometimes they discover that line by crossing it. Many times, they do so innocently, not knowing they've crossed it. That's when we end up talking about oppression.

Freud says that jokes can function to strike allegiances that unite people against a common enemy. Jokes told by those in a position of privilege or power, which target the oppressed, serve to perpetuate the oppression. Yet, often these jokes are told, by students and adults alike, without knowing how they function within the politics of humor and without the intention of causing harm. That's why we talk about it: Becoming aware of how humor works is the first step in stopping one's unconscious or unintentional participation in the oppression.

We had a spirited discussion as the students explored the workings of humor, often disagreeing with one another by pointing out the flaws in their arguments. Their engagement impressed me. They seemed genuinely interested in learning.

This discussion was especially significant within its context. These were males—a group traditionally privileged in our society—talking about the power of humor and how to use it. They seemed genuinely interested in learning how power works and what their responsibility is in wielding it.

Sitting in that classroom were tomorrow's doctors, lawyers, CEOs, and politicians—the next generation of leaders. How they use—and will use—power matters. As they become more aware of how humor works, they are more likely not to tell jokes that harm others and perpetuate oppression. They are more likely, I pray, to use power in a manner consistent with the Gospel values.

· grace ·

Words of Resurrection Amidst Suffering

Sometimes the words of resurrection come from the mouths of the suffering.

I wasn't expecting this the other evening when I called a friend who, that day, had learned the results of extensive medical tests to determine the cause of a mysterious sickness that had plagued him all winter. I was thinking of his wife and two small children and that it was unfair for someone as young and otherwise physically fit as he to be stricken with an illness. Basically, I was feeling sorry for him.

He wouldn't have any of my pity. "Suffering's not always a bad thing," he told me. "It allows God's grace into our lives."

Huh? The tests had confirmed that he suffers from a potentially debilitating illness; the treatment involves cutting back on the many interests in his busy life.

"I've been reading about Job," he said. "Often, our response to others is to want to take away their suffering, to try to solve their problem. That's what Job's friends tried to do by telling him what he'd done wrong and how he could put an end to his suffering. True compassion is entering into another's pain with them."

My friend knows. He's seen relatives die of cancer. For years, when he was single, he visited a stranger—who became a friend—in a nursing home, a middle-aged man who suffers from a crippling illness. Now he's on the other end, receiving the compassion he's given in the past. "When the phone's ringing off the hook with people who care, it's hard not to feel uplifted."

He said he feels blessed. "I felt down awhile back when I was wondering what was wrong with me. The Lord's been blessing me through this, and now I'm trying to dwell on that."

When I told him it was inspiring to hear his positive attitude, he replied without missing a beat, "That's the Holy Spirit working."

His faith impressed me as genuine and active. "This has caused me to slow down," he said. "People like me (who are successful) tend to need to get whacked upside the head before they'll make changes in their lives. I think it has drawn me closer to God."

Listening to him and his attitude drew me closer to God. I want the grace to approach suffering and adversity as he is doing, finding resurrection amidst suffering. I pass his story on to you with the hope that you'll be touched in a similar way. Tell his story to your kids. Better yet, act it out for them.

· *grace* ·

A Conversation I Never Had

The French call it *repartee d'escalier*, thinking of the perfect remark on the way down the staircase just after leaving the dinner party. Happens to me frequently, usually in the car on my drive home. One day at the end of this past school year, I was thinking of a discussion I'd had with a bright young man from Edina, Minnesota, whose political views are nearly opposite mine yet whose values seem kindred. Here's what I thought of saying to him, but never had the chance to express until now:

> You want to dismiss me as a bleeding heart, but I find in you the same trait that makes me lean toward the left—compassion. You've demonstrated your concern for others when you've stood up for your brother, whom you recognize has not been gifted as you have been.
>
> You are privileged in many ways, and because of this, you will have doors opened to you that will remain shut to others. It's not wrong to be granted such gifts and opportunities; matter of fact, it's a good thing because we need smart, compassionate people like you in positions of influence.
>
> All I ask is that when you reach that position—and along the way to getting there—please remember those who will not be able to go where you will or who will struggle more than you, those who will have to fight greater odds determined by racism, sexism, and all the other -isms that arise out of our

fears. Reach out to these others; give them a hand to help them stand on equal footing.

All this is not a matter of coming from the left or right; it goes beyond labels of liberal or conservative. It's the simple Gospel message to look beyond our own interests in the love and service of others. Our faith challenges us to look out for those who aren't similarly privileged, who are disadvantaged, who have not been granted equal opportunities.

I wish I'd said this to you—and the rest of the class—that day we disagreed, because maybe it would have allowed us to see eye to eye.

Chapter 2
When We Speak Up

Introduction

Grace happens when we speak up. When the spirit moves us to speak—and we do.

There are moments, flashes of insight or twinges of remembrance, when the teenagers in our lives suddenly seem especially dear to us. When that happens, we should tell them. It helps them realize they're lovable and loved. That love is grace.

Other times, what we've got to tell them isn't easy. Maybe it's a hard truth or bad news we're called upon to deliver. In those moments, we pray for the right words and the strength to speak them.

Our words may fall on rocky soil. We may have to repeat ourselves. We pray for patience to let the Spirit work on its own timetable.

We speak, and we listen. We let them ask their questions, which are a necessary part of navigating their way through adolescence. We recognize that they are trying to differentiate themselves from their parents by giving shape to their own experience. We resist the temptation to impose the answers we've found. We respect their process and let them find their way to answers they can trust.

We pray with our teenagers, and we pray out loud. We're laying a foundation. Even if we can't see it taking shape, we trust it will. Faith is a gift.

Throughout, we petition the Spirit to guide us. When we follow its prompting within us—to speak or to listen—we know we're moved by grace.

· grace ·

What We Love About Teenagers

The other night, when I stopped into the local Perkins restaurant, I ran into a former student who reminded me of an important lesson.

What I remembered about Ben was him reading a personal narrative to the class about a spill he took on a ski slope that sent him hurtling down the mountain out of control, very much threatening himself and others. He had the entire class laughing riotously.

I remembered how, once he got his driver's license, he'd show up breathless and several minutes late for first period, only to entertain the class with the story of that morning's driving adventure merging into rush hour traffic or trying to take a shortcut around stalled cars, which one time ended in an older driver threatening him with a hockey stick, an event that genuinely frightened Ben.

I remembered that Ben "led" the class in demerits—the way he put it, not quite the way the JROTC department characterized the frequent reprimands Ben received for wearing the wrong shoes, not shaving, or being completely out of uniform. Secretly, I applauded his rebellion, which wasn't obnoxious or malicious, but simply a quiet integrity of not going along with what didn't fit for him.

I remembered Ben as a young man full of life and spunk, with a charming sense of self-deprecating humor.

I never hear such stories in the faculty lounge; adults carry a much different energy. The delight that I took in Ben came from the sort of joy that only children deliver. That's the lesson: We need to take time to remember, especially when kids are being kids, just what it is we love about them.

There's something else, too, that we need to tell them.

I've told Ben how much I enjoy who he is. But I hope he reads this column or that someone shows it to him, so he knows that what I've said is true. I want him to be able to believe these things about himself. See, amidst the turbulent teenage years, kids forget too.

Ben left our school after his sophomore year because he'd had some sadness with his friends there. The night I saw him, in spite of his smile, I could see in his eyes the all-too-familiar insecurity and fear that tarnishes adolescence. So, I thought maybe if he could see this in print, he'd know that an adult loves him and that might make this year just a little bit easier.

That's the application of the lesson: Once we've taken time to remember the good things about the kids we love, we can help them remember.

· grace ·

Be Careful What You Say—
They Might Hear It

Are you listening to me? Ever find yourself asking a teenager this question? Sometimes, talking to a teenager seems like talking to the wind. You might be surprised to hear that they've listened.

Not long ago, I met a guy I'll call Matt in a social setting. He routinely asked where I worked. Turned out he'd attended Saint Thomas Academy, and he asked if a certain teacher still works there.

Yes, he does. "I owe my life to him," Matt said.

He went on to tell me how this teacher had persisted in trying to help him with his problems caused by alcohol and other drugs; Matt is now nine years clean and sober. He asked me to greet the teacher for him.

When I passed along the greeting and gratitude, the teacher smiled and uttered the student's nickname. "Yeah, I remember him." He told me his version, how Matt had fought everything, sworn at the teacher, and complained about his efforts. Matt had been stoned every day. The teacher told Matt that he had to get into treatment.

I imagine there were times when the teacher felt like giving up, times when he wondered what was the use, times when he figured Matt was bent upon his own destruction but damned if he'd let anyone stand in the way. There were times when he was certain Matt wasn't listening to him.

But the teacher didn't give up, and eventually the student heard him. This story might be more common than we realize.

Sure, there are times when teenagers effectively ignore us, but there are others when, even though it doesn't show at the moment, what we've said sinks in.

Raising teenagers isn't about immediate gratification. The rewards are often postponed. Even though teenagers might appear to be tuning us out, it's important to trust ourselves—and the process—and keep talking, knowing that something we say could stick.

Who knows? The Spirit works in mysterious ways.

Consider carefully what you say, but say it. They might hear.

· grace ·

Don't Lose Faith over Adolescent Agnosticism

If your teenagers claim they don't believe in God, don't worry. Could be they're simply trying to form their own faith.

Martin, a sophomore, used to question the existence of God in class. I trusted his sincerity but also suspected he merely wanted to figure out things for himself. That seems a necessary part of a teenager's faith formation: to question what one has been taught and to seek to shape one's own faith. The risk, of course, is the abandonment of what one has been taught (though that's harder to do than it sounds; more on that in a moment). More often, the result is a matured faith, grown from one's own experience and deepened by one's examination.

So, I was not surprised one morning during our prayer time at the beginning of class when Martin prayed for his ailing grandfather. A time of need seemed to bring out what he believed, and, to his credit, he was mature enough to recognize this belief and reach back to God.

While it is important to allow teenagers to question and examine their faith, it is also important not to deny our own. Even though there were those in the class who professed they did not believe, we kept saying our morning prayer.

My parents had done the same with me and my siblings when we were teenagers. They stuck with our traditional Sunday evening family prayer sessions when their three oldest children became teenagers, despite our complaints and protests. Even when one of us rebelled by staying in our room and refusing to join the prayer, my parents persisted and modeled their faith.

The result? While all four of us children struggled in some fashion during the turbulence of our teen years, we seem to have turned out okay; as adults, we all have strong faiths and have found mates with matching faiths (one of my mother's primary intentions for us).

The roots of faith my parents planted within us run so deep that my oldest sister, who as a teenager had been one of the most vocal against the family prayer gatherings, as an adult organized a family prayer meeting. Once a month, we gather to pray the rosary and offer our petitions to God.

During those times as a teenager when I rebelled and wanted to abandon my parents' beliefs, I did not think that one day I would look forward to praying with my family. Today, I recognize the value of my parents' dedication to instilling their faith in us.

So, if your teenagers are rebelling, don't lose faith, but do take comfort in knowing that it is probably a necessary part of theirs.

· grace ·

Just One Question

If you could ask God one question, what would it be? Curious about what teenagers would want to know, I asked my sophomore and senior students what they would ask God. Their responses reveal their concerns and raise challenging questions.

The most common inquiry asked, "What is the meaning of life?" Along with that, students wanted to discern their purpose with questions ranging from "What should I do as a career?" to "How do I get into heaven?"

The second most frequently posed question asked if there is indeed a heaven and if loved ones are there. Many students also wanted to know when the world would end or when they themselves would die.

There were, of course, humorous questions, my favorite being, "Paper or plastic?"

Most questions, though, were serious. Here's a sampling of the rest, any one of which would make for interesting discussion in the classroom or at the dinner table:

- Will I ever be truly happy in this world, throughout my life?
- Do all the ceremonies and regulations of the Church really make a difference in whether or not one is considered "faithful" and will go to heaven?
- When are you coming back, and what will it be like?
- When people die, do they look down upon us?

- Why do so many innocent people have to suffer from poverty, disabilities, war, and other living hells?
- Will people change and rid the world of its bigotry, environmental problems, and violence?
- Why does Jesus have only two commandments—love God and love your neighbor—yet the Church has so many?
- What does He want me to do to serve Him when I grow up?
- With respect to love of other people, how am I doing? Please explain and feel free to give suggestions. Do I know what love is?
- Are you the God all people worship, and if not, who do they worship?
- Why do You let such bad things happen to the people that I love so much?
- If you are an all-forgiving God, why is there a Hell?
- Why do You allow Satan to roam around and cause even more evil?
- What is one thing that I can do to change my life and the rest of the world for the better?
- Am I forgiven every time I repent?

These are questions that will deepen a teenager's faith. As Rainer Maria Rilke, the German poet, writes to a young poet, one must learn to love the questions themselves, because they will direct one's journey:

> Don't search for the answers, which could not be given to you now, because you would not be able to live them. And the point is, to live everything. *Live* the questions now. Perhaps then, someday far in the future, you will gradually, without even noticing it, live your way into the answer.

· grace ·

Simon Birch: Little Guy with a Giant Faith

Have you met Simon Birch? He's the lead in the eponymous movie based on the novel by John Irving, *A Prayer for Owen Meany*. Simon, like Owen, is a midget with giant faith. As a twelve-year-old, Simon believes that he is God's instrument; he's just not sure how God plans to use him. The movie follows his obsession to discover his purpose.

He turns to the local priest for reassurance that God has a plan for everyone, but the priest can't deliver—his faith doesn't run as deep as Simon's. Too bad, because Simon wants an adult to talk to. He has a friend he can talk to, but that friend lacks the experience and perspective an adult can offer. His own parents—gruff and simple—are not capable of helping him. Yet he persists in seeking out God's plan for him.

Simon, while unusual in many ways, is not so different from most teenagers. As they grapple with the question of identity, the developmental task before them, teenagers want to know how they are distinct from their parents, what makes them unique, and what their dreams are. Much of their rebellion and seemingly odd behavior during these years is actually an effort to address such questions as "Who am I?" and "What do I believe?"

Of course, they most often are not conscious of these questions. Teenagers do not get dressed in the morning thinking, "How do these clothes inform questions I have about my identity?" But these questions are there, lingering under their psyche, affecting them.

We can help, not by giving them the answers—they need to discover these on their own—but by affirming their questions, helping them frame their questions, even provoking questions. For instance, we can ask, "What is your purpose?" and "What's God's plan for you?" The more conscious they become of these questions, the closer they come to understanding who they are. Like Simon, they want this sort of direction from adults. Our faith can help us deliver.

For Simon, in the end—well, I won't tell you how the story turns out. Rent the movie or read the book. You can discuss it with your kids. Chances are, they've got questions just like Simon's.

grace

Let Me Tell You What's Right with That Picture

Many years ago, I met a man who made a lasting impression on me with his theory of how to pull a baseball player out of a batting slump. When a player is having trouble hitting the ball, the common practice is to look for the flaws in his swing. Yet, what often happens, this man said, is that the hitter ends up focusing on all that he is doing wrong and plunges deeper into the slump. His theory was to emphasize what the hitter is doing right when he does make contact and to have him visualize himself successfully building on those strengths.

This man was not a batting coach; he was a writer and teacher. I believe there's wisdom in his theory of positive reinforcement, especially when applied to teenagers.

There are times, of course, when we have to point out what a teenager has done wrong; this can be instructive to them in their own moral development. As adults, we can offer the perspective that helps them find the line between what's acceptable behavior and what's not. We can assist them in learning to connect their actions with their values by letting them know when they fall out of alignment.

Yet, we have to be careful not to get carried away with our "corrective" measures. Sometimes, it might be too easy to see the faults, causing us to miss the positive aspects of their character. How can they see their positive traits when all their mind's ear hears is our voices admonishing their defects and deficiencies? Especially during the teen years, when self-esteem is exceptionally vulnerable and not yet fully formed, we want them to be able to build on their strengths.

Pointing out faults can paralyze, while compliments can act like Miracle-Gro, helping teens flourish. With a strong self-esteem and a healthy sense of their own worth, they are more likely to be true to their values and follow their heart.

As adults, we can help move them toward this ideal of someone able to live out their faith by gently reminding them when they need correction and generously endorsing their good conduct and personal strengths. Particularly when we see them slumping, we can remember to emphasize the positive. To be on the constant lookout for this opportunity can be a form of prayer we practice with the teens we care about.

Chapter 3
When We Look for It

Introduction

Grace happens when we look for it. If we look with open eyes, we'll be amazed where we see God, how we find God, and the ways we experience God. But we have to look.

We have to allow ourselves to see what's before us in the moment.

God is there—here. God's presence permeates creation. When we look for God, we'll see God, sometimes in unexpected faces and places. That's the beauty of it. There are so many opportunities for us to stop in awe and acknowledge God's presence, even in teenagers.

Those moments we encounter God are moments of Holy Communion. They are a sacrament of grace.

· grace ·

Early Morning Snowfall

An early morning snowfall the other day left my classroom nearly empty when the bell rang to begin first period. Most of my students were still on the snowy roads. It didn't seem to make much sense to try to teach without a quorum, so we shot the breeze for a while. Days like that, when I abandon the lesson plan to talk about something significant that's happened at school or simply to hear what's on the students' minds, often turn out to be my favorite classes.

We've covered topics from dating to drinking, from getting along with parents to what's wrong (and what's right) with religion, from girls in sports to God's gender. I always try to teach some lesson or idea about the topic, so I can justify to myself that the time hasn't been wasted. I want the kids to walk away knowing just a little bit more about life, but invariably they are the ones who teach me.

The other day, probably because it was Advent, we got onto the subject of Christmas. I told them that my favorite part of the holiday is the Incarnation, the way God became one of us. This reminded one student of the country song by Collin Raye that asks what if Jesus came back as a homeless man, or an unwed mother addicted to crack.

I hadn't heard that one. But I liked the idea. Isn't the idea of Christianity to see Christ in everyone?

There have been times, often after an inspiring sermon on the subject, when I've tried—with varying degrees of success—to see Christ in my loved ones, to see Christ in my students, to see Christ in my coworkers, to see Christ in the store clerk, to see Christ in the driver who just cut me off. But, more often, I simply forget. It doesn't occur to me to look at others this way. That is, until I take the time to slow down, listen to the teenagers in my life, and be reminded by them that Christ is in each of us.

That morning it snowed, the students slowly trickled in until the class was nearly full by the end of the period. I hadn't covered the material I'd intended to teach, but that could wait until the next day. The snow taught me the importance of slowing down enough to set aside my agenda so that I can learn what's placed before me. That day, I learned to see Christ in my students.

· grace ·

Grace—More Than a Prayer Before Meals

Maybe you've seen the bumper sticker, "Grace Happens." Seems to be the antithesis of a popular cultural saying. While no one is likely to dispute the latter, I believe the former is equally true. All depends on which way we look at the glass of water.

It's there; grace is happening all around us—we just have to look for it.

When the sharp air against our cheek reminds us we're alive, when we spot the colors in clouds, when we hear the call of geese flying south, when we smell wood smoke at night, when we catch that first snowflake on our tongue—whenever nature speaks to us through our senses, that's grace happening.

When we have patience with a child, when we're able to show compassion for someone we don't like, when we have the ability to forgive that person who's hurt us, when we do a small act of kindness that goes unnoticed, when we listen without interrupting—whenever the gifts of the Spirit are active within us, that's grace happening.

When we suffer, when life goes hard, when we cry alone, when tomorrow seems worse than today, when we want to quit—whenever God does for us what we can't do for ourselves, that's grace happening.

When a baby is born, when love blooms, when a prayer is answered, when someone dies, when a child laughs—whenever we encounter the mysteries of life, that's grace happening.

When we receive the Eucharist, when a priest hears our confession, when we witness a Baptism, when we attend a wedding, when we anoint the sick—whenever Christ becomes present to us through the Sacraments, that's grace happening.

If you're looking for a way to teach your kids about gratitude, try talking to them about God's grace. They should know it's more than a prayer we say before meals.

· grace ·

Savoring Some Sage Advice from a Wise Old Monk

Years ago, when I was still a teenager, an older friend passed on to me a bit of sage advice given him by a wise monk: Every day, stop in awe of at least two things. Days I remember to do this are better days.

When and where we stop is up to us; a splendid variety of things can give us pause. Nature offers endless occasions to stand in awe, perhaps in the power of thunder or the colors reflecting off a lake's surface or the agility of squirrels clambering about trees. Beauty in its many forms, whether found in the melody of a song, the shape of a sculpture, or a great play made by an athlete (as graceful as any dance), can cause us to stop in admiration.

Other people unknowingly offer opportunities; something they do better than we can, a special talent they share, or an act of generosity can make us pause to take note. Our senses constantly offer moments to stop in awe, especially during summer, from the juice of a peach dribbling down our chin to the textures of grass, pavement, and sand we feel walking barefoot. And on and on. The opportunities waiting to stop us in awe are infinite.

Sometimes they catch my attention accidentally, when I step outside in the morning or when I'm feeling good on my bicycle. Other times, I might have to make a conscious effort to remember to look, say when I'm stuck in a traffic jam or simply having a bad day. Still other times, people offer the occasion, such as when my two-year-old niece Abby clomps across the kitchen floor wearing my sandals, or my nephew Michael takes me by the hand to show me his mother's vegetable garden blooming in the backyard, or when the priest raises the Eucharist at Mass.

Several years ago, I came across a poem that put this whole practice into perspective. When I read in George Meredith's poem "Lucifer in Starlight" the reference to God as Awe, I finally realized that all these years, whenever I stopped in awe, I had actually been acknowledging God's presence.

· *grace* ·

Finding God in Blackberries

> Earth's crammed with heaven,
> And every common bush afire with God;
> But only he who sees, takes off his shoes.
> The rest sit round it and pluck blackberries.
>
> —Elizabeth Barrett Browning

It's easy to get caught up in our routines and miss the obvious: God's presence in our midst. A poem like Elizabeth Barrett Browning's can jar us back into reality. Art has a way of speaking to our souls, luring them out of their slumber and making us feel alive again. Good liturgy does that; so, too, does a walk in the woods. To be humbled in the face of beauty brings us around to remembering we walk in God's presence.

It's when we take a moment to stop and look so that we might truly see that we notice the heaven crammed in earth, the common bushes aflame about us. Those moments are necessary to fill us up, to remind us what we're about. Once we've done so, we have more to offer the teenagers and others in our lives whom we care about.

I'm reminded of the flight instruction given to adults traveling with children: Fit your oxygen mask in place first, then help your child with his or her mask. If we do not care for ourselves, we cannot care for others. To take the metaphor a step further: If we do not draw our breath from God, we draw our breath in vain.

Without noticing the underlying reality of God's presence in our lives, we're just picking blackberries. Find God in the blackberry, and it becomes a rich spiritual experience—one we want to share with others.

· grace ·

Daily Communion's Not Just for Mass Anymore

Early one morning, I caught a glimpse of the full moon. It hung over the trees, white and round, looking like a large host suspended in the sky.

One of the benefits of being Catholic is the option to receive daily communion at Mass. Sometimes, even when we do not make it to church, God delivers. That morning, rounding a corner and coming upon the moon unexpectedly, seeing it loom above me, bone white against the early morning azure sky, was a moment of communion; God was present through the beauty of creation.

While not of the same order, this sort of daily communion can be as regular as receiving the daily sacrament. God reveals His presence in so many moments; it's simply up to us to be open to receive them.

For example, a student poked his head into my office to tell me that an injury was healing. The spontaneity of his innocent friendliness despite a stressful day offered a brief moment of daily communion. It gave me pause to smile with someone else, to be drawn outside my own worries. That respite, and the reminder of what matters most, brought me back into touch with God.

Later that day, my father called specifically to compliment me; sincere praise from our parents is always a moment of communion. An act of kindness from anyone directed toward us can be a reminder of what God has done for us simply because God so loves us and the world. God's love came through in that phone call.

Also that day, another student was nervous before giving a required speech to the class, asking me ahead of time if I thought his classmates would laugh. They didn't. They listened respectfully and said kind words to him afterward. The first student's vulnerability coupled with the other students' munificence offered a moment of daily communion under two species; I saw Christ in both.

I believe in these moments. I believe God reveals his presence in these ways and many more each and every day. I believe that when we are open to these moments and receive them, we can experience communion with God. Daily communion's not just for Mass anymore.

grace

Images of Christ

The Catholic Spirit, my local Catholic paper, ran this notice for a special section the editors planned: "We are looking for unique and powerful images of Jesus in religious art, including crucifixes, statues, stained glass, paintings, sculptures, carvings, etc." When I saw the solicitation, it stirred an image from childhood. Though not one that can be photographed, you can picture it yourself. Here is my submission of a unique and powerful image of Jesus Christ.

Back in the late sixties, when I was five years old, I injured myself on vacation, and my mother took me to the doctor. While in the waiting room, I spotted a hippie sitting cross-legged on the floor. My mother, on whose memory I rely for this anecdote, had already noticed him when he had tried, unsuccessfully, to get drugs from the nurse at the counter, and she overheard that he had been unable to provide an address. Noting the man's long hair, I leaned into my mother and whispered, "He looks just like Jesus."

Like the boy who spotted the emperor's nakedness in the famous parable, I had not yet learned to calculate the world through eyes of fear and mistrust; with the innocence of childhood, I recognized the face of Jesus.

What a shock for my mother—and for me as an adult to reflect upon it—to be jolted to a deeper understanding by a child's simple declaration of the truth.

I pass that on to you to remind myself to become once again like that child I was, able to see the face of Jesus in all God's children. Not as I expect Jesus to appear, or as I would have Him, but as Jesus is.

There's my image of Jesus, a memory. Sorry, editors, it can't be photographed. But it can be reproduced.

· grace ·

Yes, Virginia, There Is a Jesus

Over one hundred years ago, in 1897, an eight-year-old girl named Virginia, wrote a letter to the *New York Sun:* "Some of my friends say there is no Santa Claus. Please tell me the truth, is there a Santa Claus?"

In a now famous editorial, Francis P. Church replied: "Your little friends are wrong. They have been affected by the skepticism of a skeptical age. They do not believe except they see. They think that nothing can be which is not comprehensible by their little minds. . . . Yes, Virginia, there is a Santa Claus. He exists as certainly as love and generosity and devotion exist. . . ."

I thought of this during the Christmas season when I overheard several adults at lunch discussing the ages at which their children had stopped believing in Santa. I think of it, too, when I hear students deny the existence of God. What if Virginia had written instead, "Please tell me the truth, is there a Jesus Christ?"

Here's how Mr. Church might reply today.

Jesus Christ exists as certainly as love. He's in the patience a teacher shows while working with you late after school to help you understand an assignment. He's in the kindness of a small gesture, such as the driver who let your mother merge this morning during rush hour. He's in the humility of the student who picks up some paper towels off the bathroom floor and throws them in the trash without getting noticed. Yes, Virginia, there is a Jesus Christ.

He exists as certainly as generosity. He's in the older student willing to take a younger, outcast student under His wing. He's in the students who dressed up as Santa and passed out gifts to the senior citizens. He's in the young people and their families donating money and gifts to needy families selected by Catholic Charities. Yes, Virginia, there is a Jesus Christ.

He exists as certainly as devotion. He's in the grace a student says quietly to himself before eating lunch. He's in the students singing strongly at the school liturgy. He's in the Lord's Prayer said daily at Catholic schools and youth groups across the world. Yes, Virginia, there is a Jesus Christ.

He exists. He's in the birth in the manger. He's in the death on the cross. He's in the Resurrection. He's in the love in your heart, in the Eucharist on your tongue, and in the prayer on your lips.

Yes, indeed, Virginia, Jesus Christ exists. Of that you can be sure.

· grace ·

Be Not Afraid of the Kid with the Pierced Nose

When I tell adults that I teach or coach teenagers, they often respond, "I could never do that." They note how times have changed since they were teenagers, commenting on the seemingly odd habits of today's version, and conclude that they just don't understand that age. As with most prejudice, fear seems to be at the root of their uneasiness around teens; they fear what they don't understand.

Remember the story of Jesus' birth when the angel appears to a group of shepherds in the fields? The shepherds are startled, naturally, as any of us would be to suddenly have an angel of God standing among us. The first words out of the angel's mouth, Luke tells us, are, "Do not be afraid" (Luke 2:10).

Do not be afraid. Why not? Because God became human. The angel brings the Good News to the shepherds: "For today in the city of David a savior has been born for you who is Messiah and Lord" (Luke 2:11).

The angel brings the Good News of the Incarnation: God has become one of us and lives among us. Do not be afraid.

The Incarnation reflects God's immanence. No longer is God remote, present only through transcendence; God's presence has become more intimate. God dwells in each of us through the immanence of Christ.

Looking at it this way, there's no need to fear teenagers. No need to fear the unfamiliar appearances if we can remember to look for Christ within. Seeking this common ground might help us move beyond our reaction to the superficial differences, focusing instead on the good news of God's presence in each of us.

I can imagine the adults I mentioned previously stumbling over pierced body parts, baggy pants, or slang, and missing the common substance beneath that. Remember, some faithful Jews had trouble recognizing Jesus as the Messiah because He did not live up to their expectations. The Christmas season serves as a good reminder to be open to Christ's coming to—and in—all peoples. Don't be startled if today you recognize Christ dwelling among you.

Chapter 4
When We Let It

Introduction

Grace happens when we let it. We can't force grace, no more than we can force the wind to blow or the flowers to grow. We simply do our part and leave the rest to God.

Trusting God with the outcome, that's a grace itself.

So, too, is receiving the wisdom to handle a situation, which often results from heeding our intuition—the gentle guidance from within that comes from the Spirit.

Surrendering to the Spirit's direction, there's another grace.

There's plenty for us to learn in the process and no shortage of teachers. When we're ready, they will appear. We can persist in trying to impose what we want to teach them, or we can open ourselves up to what they have to teach us.

Learning from those who cross our path—grace.

Touched by grace, we're touched by God. And God's presence gives us peace. That's the gift of grace. It happens . . . when we let it.

· grace ·

An Unlikely Encounter with the Wife of Bath

The thing about grace—when you least expect it, expect it.

I can vouch for that. Happened to me in a recent interaction with a student.

Last spring, I'd been praying for wisdom—a useful quality to have in any situation but especially when dealing with teenagers.

Toward the end of the school year, I spotted Caleb, one of my students, in the hallway on a no-uniform day. His T-shirt ("Give me another beer") caught my eye. I made a mental note to ask him to turn the shirt inside out or change it. Since there was hardly anyone else in the hallway, I stopped to talk to him a moment. The week before, he'd turned in a paper about one of Chaucer's Canterbury Tales, the one told by the Wife of Bath, and he'd written that he liked her story about relationships.

To appreciate that, you have to understand Caleb. He'd be the first to tell you that he doesn't like school; he had told me that on several occasions. Usually after he'd been given a reading assignment. So, when he wrote that he liked something he read, I was delighted to hear it and told him so that day in the hallway.

He said again how much he liked the story and that it had made him think about relationships with women. He said he'd learned from her story. He even said that it changed the way he thought about women.

You can imagine my elation after struggling to show him—and other students—the value of literature, what it has to say to their lives, to hear him tell me he'd connected with something he'd read. I decided not to say anything about his T-shirt, because I didn't want to tarnish the moment by disciplining him. I wanted him to be able to walk away from our conversation with a positive feeling.

After he walked away, I realized what had happened. My prayers had been answered. For that moment, in making that decision, I'd been granted the gift of wisdom. I believe those moments, when we get the help or inspiration we need in dealing with someone, are grace.

Caleb has probably forgotten that conversation, but I haven't, because it taught me several lessons. First, to be flexible and open. Second, to accept teachable moments when they come along. And third, God answers prayers.

That moment, the inspiration to keep the conversation positive, was grace. That was God acting in me, not my own doing. I believe those are moments of God's presence, moments of God working through us. If it truly was wisdom at work, God's spirit was present. Teach me Your wisdom. . . .

· grace ·

Trusting the Force that Drives the Flower

Each spring I marvel at what Dylan Thomas calls "the force that through the green fuse drives the flower. . . ." What pushes the flower through the darkness of the soil into the light? I was pondering this, the mystery of life, one Sunday evening while watering the wild flower seeds I'd planted and wondering if they would bloom as beautifully as promised by the picture on the package.

My musings brought to mind the parable of the sower, where some of the seed falls on the edge of the path and is eaten by the birds; other seed falls on patches of rock where it finds little soil and springs up at once, but as soon as the sun comes out, the plants, not having any roots, wither; other seed falls among the thorns and is choked by them; still other seed falls on rich soil and produces its crop. Watering my wild flowers-in-waiting, I was, of course, hoping for the last option: Seeds in soil rich enough to produce a bountiful yield.

This idea turned my thoughts to raising teenagers. Often, teachers, youth workers, even parents, don't get to see the seed we sow blossom. We simply plant it, throw some water on it with a little manure (my students might say a lot of manure), but often don't know whether it takes root. The lessons we teach might not be appreciated or applied until years later.

As I was watering the bare soil hiding my seeds, I wondered whether I was wasting my time. Maybe the seed is too easily accessible to the neighborhood birds. Maybe the soil is too sandy. Maybe the weeds, which are starting to spread, will choke the young blossoms. Maybe, no matter what I do, the wild flower seeds will simply not bloom.

Sometimes, when I'm standing in front of my classes, I have this same fear. My students look bored; they lack the commitment to study seriously; they have other interests that supersede literature and composition. Maybe nothing I do will help them learn.

Finally, I concluded that it was about faith. I sow the seed, water the soil, pull the weeds—and leave the rest to God. I must trust that the force that through the green fuse drives the flower will move through my seedlings. To water and weed religiously is my act of faith. The same, I believe, holds true with my wild flowers.

· grace ·

The Teacher Will Appear Everywhere

I overheard a student, obviously defending a remark he'd made, say to another faculty member, "But he's not my teacher."

"Everyone in this building is your teacher," the teacher responded.

How true. We have something to learn from everyone. When I left Saint Thomas Academy to pursue my writing, I left with many memories of lessons others in the building, from students to fellow faculty members, taught me.

I learned humor from my students in many ways and forms, sometimes in their witty responses to questions they could not answer correctly.

I learned the importance of expressing gratitude from the students who took time to write thank-you notes.

I learned integrity from a student who pointed out a mistake I'd made in his favor when scoring a test.

I learned class from the athletes who played their hearts out on the field but stayed within the rules and showed good sportsmanship.

I learned the meaning of service from the students who willingly and happily went beyond the community service requirement because they had discovered the joy of giving.

I learned kindness in the phone message from a former student wishing me well in my new marriage after he'd heard about my engagement.

I learned compassion watching high school students play with orphaned children of Guatemala.

I learned the drive to succeed that showed in the tired faces of students who'd stayed up late—or all night—to complete homework assignments on time.

I learned about toughness in watching teenagers fight back to win a tennis match in three sets.

I learned courage from those students naming problems within their families that they were pressured to keep quiet and from those students facing their own chemical abuse.

I learned caring, patience, and compassion from other teachers in comments like the one I overheard or in direct observation of their classes.

I learned fairness from the dean in the way he treated students and dealt with the problems they presented.

I learned how to listen actively from the headmaster in his willingness to take time to hear what others had to say.

This is but a sampling of the lessons I take with me. Author Robert Fulghum learned all he needed to know in kindergarten; I find the older I get, the more I have to learn from others, especially young people. Perhaps that's why I feel an affinity with Michelangelo, whose lifetime motto was, "Ancora imparo" or, "I am still learning."

· grace ·

Something We Were Withholding Made Us Weak

Francis was a sensitive kid, perhaps too sensitive for his own good. He tried to hide behind his long hair and tattoos, but you could see the tenderness in his eyes. He felt life's pangs deeply. He tried to escape from it by smoking dope and dropping acid, but he couldn't erase his emotions. Even though his drug use drove him to living on the streets at age seventeen, he wasn't ready to quit; he wasn't ready to surrender.

I met Francis while working as a counselor in a drug treatment center. He was one of many kids whose initial infatuation with getting drunk and high had turned on them, causing a string of consequences, dragging them down into the abyss of addiction. Yet, he stood out, because there were flashes of sincerity, moments of hope when I thought he might make it, when he might bust free by accepting life on its terms. But it wasn't meant to be, not then anyway.

I last saw him ten years ago when he was being led out of the treatment center in handcuffs. He had staged a rebellion and threatened several staff members with a chrome bar pried from the towel rack. Such violence, of course, could not be tolerated.

I have inquired about him several times since, wondering what came of him. Did he end up like Jon, another boy I knew who had trouble with his temper and got shot to death in a drug deal gone bad? Did he end up like a high school pot-smoking buddy of mine who killed himself? Or, did he wind up like Marc or Shounda or David or Cindy or a host of other teenagers I've known who received God's grace through the gift of sobriety?

The gift of God's grace was there for the taking; all Francis had to do was accept it. But something—fear, or stubbornness, or pride—held him back. Robert Frost's words come to mind: "Something we were withholding made us weak, until we found out it was ourselves we were withholding from our land of living, and forthwith found salvation in surrender."

While God's ways remain a mystery to me, I have to believe that when Francis walked out of that door, my last sight of him his hands cuffed behind his back, he walked into God's care. I'm sure God didn't rescind the offer; salvation could still be Francis's, if only he would surrender. I pray he has.

· grace ·

To Thine Own Self Be True

The idea of being true to oneself is enormously popular with teenagers, especially seniors in high school. The catch, however, is that first one must know who one is.

Each year, my senior classes read Hermann Hesse's *Demian*, the story of a young man trying to discover his true self. Throughout the course of the novel, the main character, Emil Sinclair, learns to listen to his *daemon*, or, his admonishing inner voice. He slowly realizes that being true to himself means letting his *daemon* guide him.

In conjunction with the novel, we also read an article by a thirty-something woman who, by society's standards, had achieved success: She was a partner in a large law firm, traveling about the country on business, dining in the finest restaurants, and staying in the nicest hotels on a generous expense account. Yet she felt something missing. She heard an inner voice nudging her life in a different direction.

Eventually, she could no longer ignore the voice, which she identified as the Holy Spirit, and she heeded God's call to make spirituality her priority. She left her law firm, took a job with a non-profit organization, and became more involved at her church. By following the Holy Spirit in the way Sinclair follows his *daemon*, she was able to be true to herself.

Many of our class discussions focused on how to discern this inner voice—call it our *daemon* or the Holy Spirit. This voice speaks the simple truth we know when we are quiet enough to heed it, be that in prayer, in nature, during intimate conversation, participating in the liturgy, or reading the Scriptures.

That voice resides within us all. Brother Roger, the founder of Taizé, the monastery in France that attracts thousands of young people from all over the world to pray and discuss the Gospels, offers this prayer: "Christ Jesus, following you is discovering this Gospel reality: you are praying within each one of us."

Following God, earnestly listening for that inner voice, leads us to the understanding of Christ's immanence. To be true to ourselves means being true to Christ within us.

Underlying this all is the idea that God speaks directly to each of us through that inner presence. And, just as I asked my students, if God is speaking to you, what is God saying? Who does God say that you are?

grace

In the Holy Presence of God

One morning, the students, faculty, and several visitors gathered for our daily community prayer, and one of the students began, as is our custom, by saying, "Let us remember that we are in the holy presence of God."

Think about that for a moment: We are in the holy presence of God. It is so easy to interact with others, walk outdoors to and from our cars, even go through an entire day without being mindful of that reality. We may miss God's presence altogether without such a simple reminder. "Let us remember . . ." the student said, and I heard the voice of God.

Easter Sunday morning, Mary of Magdela stands outside the empty tomb weeping over the death of her friend and teacher. Jesus stands near her. But she does not recognize him; she does not realize she stands in the holy presence of God.

Rather than rejoicing at Jesus' presence, she demands of Him, thinking He is the gardener, to tell her where her friend's body is. She misses the significance of the moment. If Jesus hadn't spoken to her, she might have missed the good news altogether.

But Jesus does speak to her. "Mary," He says, and as soon as He has spoken her name, she recognizes Him. It is then, at that moment, that she realizes the truth: Christ is risen. We stand, as Mary does, always in the presence of the risen Christ. Our God lives among us.

Yet, how easy, like Mary, to miss that fact at first. God calls our name in so many ways. After this morning's prayer, I tried to be more attentive to God's presence among us. When a student approached me in the hallway, I remembered what I'd heard at prayer and tried to listen more closely. When I saw the late afternoon light slant over the trees, I appreciated God's beauty in nature. I even think I glimpsed God's presence with the two teenaged lovebirds kissing under a tree by the lakeshore.

Later in the Gospel of John, when the disciples tremble with fear behind locked doors, Jesus makes his holy presence known to them, saying, "Peace be with you" (John 20:21).

Awareness that we are in the holy presence of God brings that gift: the peace of Christ.

Chapter 5
When We See Beyond Stereotypes

Introduction

Grace happens when we see beyond the stereotypes; when we seek the substance behind the appearance.

Of course, where teenagers are concerned, it's easy to get caught up in appearances. We see baggy pants, long hair, tattoos, pierced body parts—and want to write them off. Wait a minute. What's inside?

That kid with the nasty scowl has a sensitive side. That long-haired kid teaches Confirmation classes. That football player wants to be a priest. Grace lets us see that; grace lets us glimpse their faith.

Stereotypes don't stop with teenagers. We slap them on whatever's unfamiliar, unknown, suspicious. We shape language to reinforce our fears and suspicions.

Teenagers see right through this. And they'll tell us. Knock off the prejudice. Get real. They demand we look beyond the stereotypes.

A popular rock band takes its name and inspiration from a Baptist woman who makes them promise to be good. They do. Things aren't always as they seem. Grace lets us see them as they are.

Grace leads us to the truth.

· grace ·

They'll Know Us by Our Children's Faith

One year, during our celebration of Catholic Schools Week, the visiting priest who said our all-school Mass challenged us: "Would a visitor to Saint Thomas Academy know your school to be Catholic?" I pass the challenge on to you: Would a visitor to your home know your family to be Catholic?

The visitor might notice the crucifix on the wall, the picture of the pope, or the rosary lying about, but these are merely outward signs of Catholicism. He or she would know our faith by the actions of our children.

Now, I want to be quick to clarify that not all actions by children, especially teenagers, reflect upon their parents or teachers; rebellion is universal and nondenominational. It's just when I look at the positive things some teens do, I can only think that it's a result of the faith they've been raised with.

If you were to walk into Saint Thomas Academy, you'd meet students who take service trips to Guatemala and Chicago, who wake up early Thanksgiving morning to deliver turkeys, who drive miles to play Santa for nursing home residents, who put in numerous service hours for various local charities, who plan student masses and prayer services, who attend daily Mass, who pray on their own, who fill boxes with clothes and canned goods for the needy, who organize all sorts of charitable drives, and who do many other good deeds that go unnoticed. They're not perfect kids—they spit and swear and make mistakes like other kids (and like any of us)—but they do practice their faith, and it's evident.

Many a good parent's Catholic faith is evident in their teenager's actions elsewhere, as well. I think of Nick, a public school student I knew years ago. You might not guess his faith by looking at him—a scrawny, misfit-looking kid with long hair (once dyed black, later bleached), and regularly attired as though ready to attend a rock concert, or just back from one. He was honest, trustworthy, humorous, sensitive, and caring. He taught Sunday School and led retreats for kids preparing for Confirmation. By the time he graduated, he had one of the most mature faiths of any student I've known. Those who got to know him got to see his faith—and the faith of his parents.

Still wondering how your faith might fare? In another sermon at another church, another priest talked about the importance of teaching children to pray. He said one test of how well parents have done raising their children is how comfortable they would feel asking any of their children to say grace with a guest at the table.

The challenge before us who interact with teenagers is to put our faith into their practice.

· grace ·

Beauty and the Beast

Nate's a tough-looking kid. He flashes a nasty scowl backed by a muscular build. He's the kind of kid to whom you'd give up your seat on the bus or who you'd let cut in front of you in the lunch line. One look from him can be that convincing.

He's the kind of kid you might easily misjudge. Looking at him, you might miss his sensitivity and compassion for others. Let me illustrate by sharing with you his thoughts.

Over Christmas break, Nate attended the play *Beauty and the Beast* with his grandma. Afterward, he wrote a paper describing the play and its theme—Never judge a person because of how they look:

> To me, this theme is relevant every day. I meet people all of the time, and I still occasionally judge people from what they look like. It is human nature to form an opinion based on your reaction to a first impression. First impressions are more often mostly based on looks, rather than character. This story was created as a reminder to me to step back and try to listen to what a person has to say, then build my opinion based on what that particular person stands for.

Maybe this idea jumped out at him because of his own experience of being judged by his looks before he could be given a chance to prove himself. It could've been a bus driver who misread his expression or simply an adult who doesn't like teenagers.

Whatever Nate's experience has been, the play made enough of an impression on him that he resolved to himself that he would wait to learn what the next person he met was about instead of immediately slapping a label on him or her. "It might be human nature to label people, but that does not mean we cannot evolve out of that 'herd instinct,'" Nate wrote.

He'd taken the play's theme to heart and passed on its message with a powerful example of how to live it.

I've met a lot of Nates in my day—teenagers I initially was tempted to write off because of the way they looked or giggled in groups or fell asleep in class or drove too fast. Upon further inspection—once I got to know them—I was able to see the goodness lurking within, only waiting for the right moment to come out. I'm sure you've met your share of Nates, too. Matter of fact, you're likely to meet one today.

grace

Permeated with the Gospel Spirit

The other day I found myself talking to a young man who did not want to be at Saint Thomas Academy. He wanted to go to a public school that does not have a military department, that does have girls, and where his friends won't each come from a different zip code. What he'll give up, though I don't think he realizes it, is the Catholic dimension.

This is the part of a Catholic school many students take for granted—those who think what makes the school Catholic is the required religion classes. They miss the subtle but firm foundation of faith that shapes a Catholic school's identity.

Beyond the crosses hanging in each classroom, the Catholic identity of the school should be present in everything we do. It is our *raison d'etre*, it's what makes us what we are and what distinguishes us from other schools. This difference—experiencing the daily practice of gospel values—should be palpable to students.

Perhaps the following quote, which our headmaster read to the faculty early in the school year (though I don't otherwise know its origin), says it best: "From the first moment that a student sets foot in a Catholic school, he or she ought to have the impression of entering a new environment, one illuminated by the light of faith and having its own unique characteristics, an environment permeated with the Gospel spirit of love and freedom."

To create—and preserve—such an environment in our schools and in our homes is the responsibility of each of us. We each have a part in the first and lasting impression our schools make, and we might give pause to consider how we're handling that responsibility.

Maybe the student thinking of transferring will recognize how our school is different when he leaves, in much the same way we begin to appreciate something—know it for what it was—only after we've lost it. But by then, it will be too late. It's up to us to show him now, so that he can appreciate what he's got before he loses it.

· *grace* ·

Sister Hazel: Promise to Be Good

At the 1999 Basilica Block Party, within the wave of college-age kids pressing toward the outdoor stage, one mother and her son stood their ground, singing along to the rock group Sister Hazel. They'd waited months for this chance, both being big fans, but eleven-year-old Grant was too young to get into the other traditional venues around town where the band has played. An unusual sight in many ways: mother and son at a rock concert, and a rock concert at the church. But then, Sister Hazel is an unusual band.

This is not a rage-against-the-machine, friend-of-the-devil type band. They're a group of guys from Gainesville, Florida, who named their band after a hometown woman (not a nun, as the name might suggest, but a Baptist) legendary for her good works. Their CD liner notes explain that Sister Hazel's Rescue Mission "gave those who were down on their luck a safe place to stay warm, eat and regroup regardless of age, race or beliefs. It is in this spirit of unconditional concern for all beings that we have chosen to use her name."

So you see, it's not so unusual to find Sister Hazel performing at the Basilica, since their philosophy resonates with the Church's social ministry. The band supports and promotes several charities, including Big Brothers-Big Sisters of America, Make-A-Wish

Foundation, the American Cancer Society, and the American Foundation for AIDS Research.

But a mother and a son liking the same band? For Grant, it's simple: He likes their sound. His mom likes what the band stands for and sees them as positive role models. Now, that's unusual for a rock band.

Yet this band reflects family values that a mother can trust. In the liner notes for Sister Hazel's second CD, each member individually thanks his parents and dedicates his music to God or his family. Ken Block, the lead singer, knows the value of family: When he was in his late teens, he lost his little brother, Jeffrey, to leukemia, an experience he sings about in the song "Running Through the Fields." Rather than growing bitter, Ken went on to get his master's degree in psychology and headed up a chapter of Big Brothers-Big Sisters before his band made it big.

As Grant sang along at the concert, he wore a Sister Hazel T-shirt that Ken had autographed before the show with a marker he carries for that very purpose. He'd written, "Grant, Be good." Not long ago, Sister Hazel agreed to let the band use her name if *they* promised to be good. So far, they're making good on their promise.

· grace ·

Huckleberry Finn and the Power of Words

Each year, the sophomores read *Huckleberry Finn*, a book Ernest Hemingway praised as one of the finest books in American literature, yet one that's offensive for its repeated use of the word *nigger*. The challenge in teaching the novel is to expose the students to its virtues—which are numerous—while at the same time acknowledging its shortcomings and not promoting bigotry. The sophomores demonstrated to me once again that they're capable of discerning good from bad, even within one book.

Rather than ignore what was offensive, we discussed the power of language. We started by making a list of derogatory words like the n-word. There was one for nearly every marginalized group in our society.

When asked what the words in the list had in common, the sophomores quickly identified the terms as stereotypes with negative connotations—terms rooted in ignorance and fear. When asked the function of these words, they again quickly identified how these terms serve as put-downs—an effort to build up oneself at the expense of another.

Each time I've done this exercise over the past several years, the students have gone on to identify how words can depersonalize and dehumanize people. They've pointed out how in wartime, words ascribed to the enemy make it easier to kill a "jap" or a "gook" than a person from Japan or North Vietnam. They've even explained how it's easier to justify the genocide of "kikes" than the mass murder of the Jewish people.

The power of words does not end there, though. Words can be used to love, to heal, to create, to compliment, to apologize, to forgive, to pray, to thank, to motivate, to enlighten, and even to change bread and wine into the body and blood of Jesus Christ. It all depends on what words we use and how we use them.

Huckleberry Finn, the novel, is not perfect, just like its hero is not. But reading the novel allows us the opportunity to discuss issues and values. It allows us the opportunity to offer a Catholic perspective and suggestions for how to apply the Gospel values.

When we finished our discussion about words that afternoon, one of the students asked, "Are you going to write about us in your column?" Yep. I wanted to give you the chance to continue the discussion at home. How do you use words?

· grace ·

I Say Football Player, You Say—What?

Let's play a little word association: Football player—quick, what words pop into your mind? Did *sensitive*, *reverent*, *holy*, *caring*, or *living* make your list? If not, I wish you could have attended our first school Mass. Our football players were all these things and more when they put on that liturgy.

The quarterback, one of the team captains, introduced the liturgy with an invitation to all—especially those who are not Catholic—to join in the prayer. That right there set the tone. Not just because the quarterback happens to be Jewish, but more so because he happens to be one of the most respected kids in the school. The other kids readily joined him in prayer.

A linebacker sang a solo. A nose guard gave me Communion. Others read from the Scriptures, offered intercessions, brought up the offertory gifts, and so on.

Courage may have been on your list of a football player's attributes. Each who was involved demonstrated courage by taking the risk of getting up to participate in front of his peers. Unfortunately, liturgies in high school are not considered as cool as, say, football games. The football team may have changed that.

Powerful probably made your list. Football players have tremendous influence without our community.

They serve as role models—even heroes. When they took charge of the Mass, they transformed the way other students perceive school liturgies. Their courage and example made Mass cool.

I was delighted. This is what we are about as a Catholic school. Just a day earlier, in my third-period English class, the seniors were complaining about having God and religion crammed down their throats. Then, there they were, running the show, celebrating the Eucharist as they saw fit.

I have been proud of our guys when I watched them on the field, reviewed highlight tapes with them, and read in the daily newspaper about their success, but I was proudest of them during that Mass. As far as I am concerned, that was their greatest victory of the season.

Chapter 6
When We Serve

Introduction

Grace happens when we serve others. And when we let them serve us. Both require a humility that puts us in touch with a love greater than ourselves. We recognize that love as coming from God.

Love takes many forms, service being one of them. So, too, service can take many forms. Sometimes it can be as grand as missionary work, sometimes as simple as sitting beside another person as Mother Teresa did. Small acts of kindness can inspire larger ones in others.

We can't give away what we haven't got, so, if we desire to love, we must fill ourselves with love. Only then can we do as the Dalai Lama exhorts: To love each person we meet. Gandhi drives home the point: If you can't find God in the next person you meet, you need look no further. These models of love inspire us to serve those we love.

Having someone to serve is a grace itself. Those people in our lives, including our teenagers, allow us to practice love. That's grace at work.

· grace ·

Reverse Missionary Work

On a cold January day, a group of ten teenagers from Saint Thomas Academy boarded a plane headed for Guatemala, where they planned to volunteer for ten days on a service project. Earlier that month, twelve students from Cretin-Derham Hall returned from Guatemala. Other groups of teenagers like them will travel to Guatemala through the course of the year.

They traveled to San Lucas Toliman, a tiny mountain town snugged on the shores of Lago Atitlan, where they stayed at the mission of Fr. Greg Schaefer, a Minnesotan priest stationed in San Lucas. There, they spent their time picking coffee, clearing fields, digging ditches, laying pipes, or doing whatever other work needed to be done that week. They played with orphans, visited scenes of "the violence" (Guatemala had perhaps the bloodiest of all Central America's civil wars, claiming hundreds of thousands of lives), worshipped in the local church, and passed time with the locals.

Most importantly, they would come back and talk about what they saw and did. They would tell their friends about the site in Santiago Atitlan where the government death squad shot dead Fr. Stan Rother and how they saw his bloody handprints that still stain the wall. They would tell their families about the coffee co-op and how it benefits the people who grow and pick the coffee.

Father Schaefer calls it reverse missionary work, letting people back home know what the missionaries are doing and why they're needed. He has hosted thousands of visitors over his forty years in San Lucas—housed them, fed them, educated them, and sent them home—so they can spread the word to those who can't come visit or may be inspired to once they hear of it. (That's how it worked for me: I'd heard of his mission from many friends who'd been there and finally visited myself last year with a group of students.) The idea is that the better we know a place, the closer it is to us, the more we will care about it and see the similarities we have with other people. That way, the people on both ends benefit.

The teenagers traveling there have their work cut out for them when they return: to educate us. By sharing their experience with us, they will be doing the missionary work of teaching us the lessons they've learned.

Thinking about that, I realize they need not to have traveled to another country to do so.

grace

Dalai Lama Love

The Dalai Lama said the secret to inner peace lies in the decision to love every person we meet.

Easier said than done. So how to do that?

I think of Levin in Tolstoy's novel *Anna Karenina* (my favorite novel). After Kitty expresses her love to him, Levin is filled with happiness. He's in an exalted mood and feels love for everyone he meets—from the coachman to his contemporaries—seeing each as good and kindhearted. He even feels love for a man he once resented: "Levin was completely incapable of understanding or recalling why he had ever been annoyed with Sviyazhsky, or what he had failed to find in him. He was an intelligent and wonderfully kindhearted fellow."

Levin, filled with the love another feels for him, is able to love others. He's found the secret that makes possible what the Dalai Lama does; he's found love.

So what does this have to do with teenagers? Everything. Whether we teach or parent them, we're trying to love them. Sometimes, as anyone who's tried knows, that's easier said than done.

So, how to do that? We do what Levin does: We go to the source. We first fill ourselves with love so that we have something to share.

Maybe you go to your spouse, maybe to your friends. Maybe you go to Mass, maybe to a Bible study. Maybe you go to the woods, maybe to the lake. Doesn't matter where you go, so long as that's the place that fills you up. Wherever you go, if it's love you're getting, the source is the same. What's important is to go to it and drink deeply, to fill yourself with love.

Once we're feeling loved, like Levin, we're more likely to see the goodness in others and be able, like the Dalai Lama, to love those we meet.

· grace ·

Mother Teresa's Ministry of Presence

I learned of Mother Teresa's death from the students as they trickled into my seventh-period class. After a moment of silence, we discussed her humility and greatness. From their comments, I was again struck by the tremendous impact of this small woman's big life. She is a model of spirituality and faith for us all.

Mother Teresa's ministry lives well beyond all the eulogies bestowed on her those weeks following her death in 1997.

An anecdote I heard epitomizes Mother Teresa's ministry.

Shortly after she heard the call to follow Jesus to the slums to serve him among the poorest of the poor, Mother Teresa came upon a woman half-eaten by maggots and rats lying in the street in front of a hospital. Mother Teresa sat with the woman until she died.

She sat with her. That's all. She didn't heal her. She didn't carry her inside the hospital. She didn't rail against the powers responsible for the woman's poverty. She offered her all she had: Her presence. She sat with her. That was Mother Teresa's calling— the ministry of presence.

Isn't this often what our teenagers wish from us? Not always, of course. There are plenty of times when they want their privacy or want to be left alone with their friends. But I believe they desire from us, as adults who care about them, the same sort of presence Mother Teresa offered. They want us to sit with them. To affirm who they are, to show them we care, to accept them—with our presence. Whether as a parent, teacher, coach, or simply as an adult, when we listen to them without judging, when we let down our guard to laugh with them, when we attend their games and performances—we minister with our presence.

There's more they need from us, sure, but sometimes our presence means more than we realize.

I'm struck by how much Mother Teresa's ministry resembled Jesus'. Yes, He preached, healed, and redeemed, but His, too, was a ministry of presence. Witness the Incarnation, God made human. He stooped from heaven to sit with us.

Every time we partake in the Eucharist, we're offered a reminder of Jesus' ministry. Every time we practice this ministry of presence with others, we once again participate in the Real Presence.

May the memory of Mother Teresa live on in our practice.

· *grace* ·

Students Complete Us

Each fall, we start the school year without the students. The days before classes begin are a time for teachers to sort textbooks, organize classrooms, compare notes, prepare lessons, and attend in-services. The desks are empty, the classrooms barren. Hallways ring with a vacant echo.

While the days are busy, filled with anticipation for the coming week and the rush to get ready, there's something palpably missing. Without the students, the school has no pulse. Their return transforms the building; their presence brings it to life. Once again, it's a school.

A student once gave a stirring speech that Saint Thomas is not the building you see from the freeway when driving by; Saint Thomas is the community gathered in the court listening to his speech. Just as we, the people, are the church, so are we the school. Together, we form community.

Another way of looking at it is that the students complete us. Without students, you can't have teachers. They are our complement.

Even more than that, though, the students remind us why we're here. They provide us with purpose. At some point, we made the decision—as teachers or parents—that we were going to serve them. In doing so, our lives become meaningful. Service grants us our place within community.

That can also offer us perspective. While the first weeks of school carry an excitement and provide the opportunity to begin anew, as the year wears on, we grow tired as teachers and parents. Looking ahead to the next vacation, we may miss the moment. We're likely to forget our patience. We're likely to grumble about the work.

That's when it will be useful to remember those early days, when the school—and our purpose—felt empty. We look to the students, and they remind us why we're here.

· grace ·

A Little Ice Cream Goes a Long Way

Another teacher told me a story I want to pass on to you.

On a trip to a third world country, a high school student, disturbed by the widespread poverty he saw, felt sympathy for the people he met and wondered what he could possibly do to make a difference.

One evening when his group went to Häagen-Dazs, this teenager saw a small girl begging in the street. He approached her and asked what flavor of ice cream she liked best. Then, he went inside, bought a cup of ice cream that flavor, picked up two spoons, and returned to the girl. He sat on the curb with her, eating the ice cream and talking to her.

He did this because it seemed the right and kind thing to do, not to impress anyone. He had no idea his teacher would tell me about it or that I would tell you. He had no idea how far-reaching his action might be. But I believe his action does reach beyond that evening and that little girl.

When I heard this story, I was touched by this young man's selflessness, compassion, and sharing. That's why I pass it on to you; I imagine you'll be touched by it as well. Sometimes a small action can have a widespread impact. While I'm sure this teenager did not realize it when he asked that little girl what her favorite ice cream flavor was, he'll realize if he sees this that a little bit of goodness can go a long way.

These days, as young people ask one another What Would Jesus Do? one of them unintentionally has provided us with an answer. Back in His day, Jesus multiplied bread and fish to share with others. Had He met that little girl, I think He would have bought her ice cream. Come to think of it, maybe He did.

· *grace* ·

The Grace to Let You Be My Servant

I remember a school Mass when we sang "The Servant Song" by Richard Gillard. It was the same Mass when we heard the story of Jesus washing feet. The first verse goes: "Will you let me be your servant, let me be as Christ to you; Pray that I may have the grace to let you be my servant, too."

The last part is easier sung than done.

The model of Jesus humbling himself to wash the disciples' feet has served as an inspiration for service ranging from daily acts of kindness to a lifelong commitment of ministering to others. Yet, Peter objected to having his feet washed by the Lord. Why?

Serving others, paradoxically, often comes in the form of authority—as with a teacher, parent, priest, or otherwise—and puts us in control. Reversing the roles takes away that control and makes us vulnerable. Being served is not always comfortable; it involves humility—the trust to let go of control.

The humility required to be served can enable us to see Christ in others as the server. At Communion during that school Mass, I found myself in a line being served by a student with whom I'd had a conflict.

Perhaps Peter, in my shoes, would've considered switching lines. My pride made me think about it, but, at the same time, I didn't want to shun this student.

In retrospect, I'm grateful I didn't switch lines because I would have missed a moment of grace. As the student extended the host and I accepted the Body of Christ, we were both touched by the humility that makes reconciliation possible.

After that, I looked at that student in a different light, and our relationship improved. Perhaps not all times that we have the grace to let others be our servants will be as poignant, but these moments certainly have the potential to reveal Christ's presence.

Chapter 7
When We Are Grateful

Introduction

Grace happens when we're grateful, which means more than saying thank you.

Once a year, at Thanksgiving, we take stock of all our blessings that inspire gratitude. But when we practice this attitude of gratitude throughout the year, we find that it changes our outlook. We start looking for opportunities to be grateful. We thank God for whatever water we find in the glass.

Two special blessings beg our gratitude—parents and children. We should let them know we appreciate them while we still can. A wise teenager who'd lost his father taught me that. That's a lesson I'm grateful for and one I try to apply regularly.

Sometimes we don't appreciate others except in hindsight. That can happen with our own parents. Not until we're doing for someone else what our parents did for us do we appreciate all they did. If we're lucky, it's not too late to thank them. We can also be grateful for the way their generosity reflects that of our heavenly Parent.

Gratitude has the power to change our lives. That's grace.

· grace ·

Hug Your Kids

Sometimes I grow tired of teaching high school seniors. They're at that stage when they've got all the answers—or so they think. I remember being there myself, thinking I knew it all, pitying the adults for their ignorance. Today, I realize how little I know—and how much teenagers have to teach us.

Recently, Ryan taught me about gratitude.

One of the traditions at Saint Thomas Academy is that each senior gives a speech to the entire student body. Ryan gave his speech on the one-year anniversary of his father's death.

He described the morning he heard the news, how he'd seen his mother crying at the breakfast table, how he'd gone up to his parents' bedroom and found the bed where his father had spent the last weeks of his life neatly made—empty. He told us that sometimes we don't fully appreciate those we love until we lose them.

Here's a kid eighteen years old and wise. He spoke with authority, having gained his wisdom through his suffering. He taught me to be grateful for those I love. And for those who teach me. Thanks, Ryan.

I learned something else that day from the other students. Seven hundred boys, ranging in age from twelve to eighteen, stood and listened to Ryan. They didn't laugh, poke fun, or screw around. They showed him respect. They impressed me with their compassion.

Ryan went on to say that he had no regrets. During his father's illness, he'd been able to tell him he loved him and say goodbye. But, he said, there are times when he misses his dad and wishes he could hug him once more. He asked the other students to go home that day and hug their parents for him.

I cried. Don't you get tears in your eyes just hearing about it? Such pain, yet such maturity. And such wise words.

Hug your parents, if you still can. Tell them you love them.

And hug your kids. Be grateful for who they are today.

· grace ·

Share the Fruits of Generosity

Parents amaze me—the way they're constantly giving to their children. Their generosity teaches me what love is.

I see it in the sacrifices parents of my students make to send their children to a private, Catholic school. I see it in the time my friends devote to their young children. I see it in the ongoing care my parents continue to extend to their adult children.

I didn't always see this. During my late teen years, distracted by my own troubles, I focused on my parents' faults. I could see little else. And I didn't hesitate to remind them of what I saw.

Sadly, I recognize by the comments some of my students make that they've found that phase, too. Yet, for their sake and their parents', I hope it is only a phase.

It seems that along with maturity comes the blessing of being able to focus on one's parents' strengths and gifts. Looking back, I see how over the years my parents have been amazingly generous, whether it be providing for me or forgiving me for my teenage shortsightedness. (As a side note, it's also amazing how contemplating another's strengths obscures that person's weaknesses and improves a relationship.)

While I'm grateful for all that my parents have given me, especially the gift of faith, I'm particularly grateful for the model of their generosity. Whether the Thanksgiving season or another time of year, it seems fitting to practice what our parents have taught us. Just as the settlers and American Indians generously shared the fruits of their harvests, so, we too, can share the fruits of our parents' generosity with them and others.

To take it a step further, our heavenly Parent is the prototype of generosity, as John 3:16 reminds us: "For God so loved the world that he gave his only Son, so that everyone who believes in him may not perish but might have eternal life." There's an amazing love for which we can be grateful and which we can share generously.

That's enough to enable us to reflect on God's amazing love.

· grace ·

Adopting an Attitude of Gratitude

In the program of Alcoholics Anonymous, members sometimes refer to the program's initials as an abbreviation for what is really required of the recovering alcoholic if he or she is going to find peace in sobriety: An attitude adjustment. Many alcoholics and addicts, through the course of their addictions, have developed a cynicism toward themselves and others; they have become bitter and resentful toward themselves, others, and God. Such a negative orientation, needless to say, will not lead to serenity. They need an attitude adjustment.

The program recommends adjusting to an "attitude of gratitude." By taking stock of the positive aspects of life, expressing gratitude toward others and situations rather than blaming and resenting them, the recovering alcoholic starts to see the many blessings and joys in his or her life. For example, a difficult situation at work is not seen as an excuse to gripe in the company cafeteria, but as an opportunity for growth discussed at one's meeting.

Rob is one of those kids who was able to make that adjustment. When I met him as a patient at the residential in-patient treatment center where I worked, he was an angry guy—angry at the police who had arrested him, angry at his parents for putting him in treatment, angry at coaches and teachers he thought hadn't given him a fair chance. He was angry at the world and wanted to fight it.

As Rob slowly made the connection between his drinking and his consequences, he also came to the understanding that his attitude was responsible for much of his unhappiness. It's hard to be happy when you're out to get even with the world. With time, as he softened and let in those who wanted to help, he shifted from blaming others to accepting responsibility for his actions. Then he got in touch with God and started to appreciate the good things in his life—his loving family, his athletic and intellectual abilities, his opportunities to study and travel, even his disease. He got sober.

Though I've lost touch with Rob over the years, the last time I saw him he was full of gratitude and faith. I've heard he's staying sober through the grace of God and his own gratitude.

Personally, I feel grateful to have been able to watch this miracle of transformation occur. Telling you about Rob reminds me what a difference an attitude of gratitude can make in our lives.

· grace ·

My Dad Was Always There

My dad was always there, at every football, baseball, basketball and hockey game; at every swimming meet and tennis match. He was there at my brother and two sisters' games, matches, and meets. He was there at dance and piano recitals and class plays. All told, he spent thousands of hours attending our events. He provided us his presence.

In addition, he offered us guidance without pushing us; he paid for our equipment, lessons, and entry fees; he congratulated us in victory and consoled us in defeat; he spent hours playing catch and pitching batting practice; he chauffeured us to and from games and practices; and he even took his turn coaching.

Yet, as a teenager, there were times when I was not satisfied with all that and wanted more from him. When a ground ball passed between my legs, for instance, or I got cut from a team, I wished he'd been a star athlete himself and passed on more athletic genes to me.

That's all part of growing up, I suppose, wanting something more from our parents and missing all they have given. Seems once we reach that age of detecting our parents' defects, we blame them for their effects on us. Teenagers, especially, struggle with this, as their childhood vision of their parents as perfect gives way to the reality of who they are, flaws and shortcomings included. Many times, teenagers struggle to accept their parents for who they are, perhaps even feeling betrayed by their parents for being human and having faults.

My poor dad—he suffered for my shortsightedness as I fixated on his flaws and forgot all that he'd given me. I've seen other parents suffer in this way, mainly at the words and actions of their disgruntled teens. It is not a pretty sight—nor a pleasant feeling, I'm sure, for any parent who has born the brunt of their child's judgment.

As I aged and gained a better understanding of the world, I found peace in accepting my father as he is. I also realized that my expectations at times were unrealistic and unfair. Most important, I've learned to be grateful for what he gave me instead of regretting what he couldn't give.

I guess I learned how to do that from my father, too. He had many reasons to be critical of his own father, an alcoholic, but I never heard my father speak poorly of him. I only wish I hadn't been so quick to do so myself; my father deserves my gratitude. Being able to see that now, I believe, is another gift, this one from the heavenly Father, one I pray your own teenagers will receive—with time.

· *grace* ·

Remember to Say Thanks

Every now and then a student returns to say thank you. Jesus complained when only one of the ten He had healed was moved by gratitude to come back and thank Him (Luke 17:11–19), but any middle or high school teacher would be happy with those numbers. Parents might consider themselves lucky if their teenagers thanked them for one out of every ten things they did for their children. That's why, when one does say thank you, the gratitude expressed can mean so much.

This thought occurred to me one day when watering a plant a student had given me several years ago. Stephanie had enclosed a note with the plant thanking me for being her teacher—a gesture completely unexpected but greatly appreciated. I'm not sure I ever thanked her for that.

Matter of fact, I'm not sure I ever let Stephanie know how much I appreciated her. She was a wonderful student and a nice person. A gifted writer, she took the creative writing elective I taught—twice. I could've thanked her for that, or for staying up late to finish her assignments, or for taking her studies seriously, or for showing an interest in learning, or for speaking up in class, or for sharing her gifts with the rest of us, especially her creativity—she was easily one of the best writers in the class both years. I could've thanked her for being courteous and honest and funny and smart.

Maybe I simply expected all this of her, so I didn't think to thank her for any of it. Perhaps that's the reason we don't hear those words often enough from teenagers. Sure, they probably expect of us all that we do for them. But maybe if we showed them more often our gratitude, said thank you more often ourselves, we'd see and hear more of their gratitude.

Thanks for the plant, Stephanie, and for everything else.

Chapter 8
When We Enter into Life's Mysteries

Introduction

Grace happens when we enter into life's mysteries. We don't approach them as Sherlock Holmes, but more as John of the Cross. Life's mysteries are not to be solved; they're to be contemplated. In doing so, we enrich our faith.

So much cannot be explained. Or grasped. From the migrating bird to the empty tomb, we simply stand in awe. Rather than dismiss what we can't know, we embrace it, and enter into the mystery. That's a form of prayer.

The Christian mysteries are like Zen koans. They bend the mind and inform the soul. That enlightens our faith.

Perhaps my favorite mystery is the Resurrection. The death and life cycle touch our lives in so many ways, from actual deaths to small moments of rebirth, from nature around us to love transforming us. It seems to me that one could live a full and happy life in constant contemplation of the Resurrection. That would be a rich prayer indeed.

Teenagers themselves often seem a mystery. To embrace them, rather than try to solve them, can be a moment of grace that fills us with Christ's presence.

Grace, too, is a mystery. We can't explain the moments when it arrives, just simply embrace them when it does.

· *grace* ·

The Migrating Bird Leaves No Trace

> The migrating bird
> leaves no trace behind
> and does not need a guide.
>
> —Robert Bly Dogen

This Zen master's meditation came to mind when twice in one day I spotted a monarch butterfly. As you probably know, monarchs are famous for their migrations, traveling hundreds of miles in large packs to the extreme south of the United States, even as far as Central and South America. In the spring, they return home, lay their eggs, and die.

These little creatures leave no trace behind in their migration, nor do they need a guide to show them the way. Somehow, they travel incredible distances with unerring precision. How?

It's one of the mysteries of life—not to be solved so much as to be marveled at. That, to me, seems the spirit of the poem from Dogen, who taught a form of Zen practice that emphasizes quiet meditation.

The twentieth century American lay Catholic may have more in common with this Japanese Buddhist monk from the thirteenth century than we'd initially think. Both he and we are immersed in the mysteries of life. Our faith, too, contemplates the mysteries of life, not as an effort to solve them, but as a means of appreciating the awesomeness of God,

From the birds in the air to the flowers in the field, the mystery of life surrounds us. That calls to mind another mystery—God's love for us, as Jesus reflects in another passage about birds: "Look at the birds in the sky; they do not sow or reap, they gather nothing into barns, yet your heavenly Father feeds them. Are you not more important than they? Can any of you by worrying add a single moment to your life-span?" (Matthew 6: 26–27) The message seems to be trust the mystery. It works for the birds and butterflies; surely, it will work for us.

When we meditate upon the mysteries about us, they remind us that we are part of the mystery, which is not cause for concern but a source of comfort.

grace

Never Underestimate a Mother's Prayers

My mother used to tell me, "Never underestimate the power of prayer." I don't, especially hers. My mother's prayers for me have been granted so many times over the years that I do not doubt their power; she's made me a believer.

Understand, she's a woman of deep faith who reserves time daily to pray, but she's also a mother, and, like Mary, I believe as such she enjoys special intercessory privileges. Now, I'm not putting her on the same level as the Queen of Saints, nor do I mean to compare myself to Mary's son. What I'm saying is that mothers seem to have some powerful pull with their prayer.

While I'm grateful for the many blessings that have come my way as a result of my mother praying the rosary, I'm especially grateful for her prayer efforts for my sobriety. See, when I was a teenager, my mother had much occasion for prayer on my behalf.

My mother did all she could for me as a parent—so did my father—but she recognized her limitations, as most parents of teenagers are forced to, especially those whose children are abusing chemicals. She knew she needed divine assistance, so she turned to God.

The power of her prayer worked in spite of me. I was intent on destroying myself, as most addicts are. But she persisted. Despite the frustration caused by my behavior and God's seeming reluctance to intervene, she never gave up on me or on God. She kept praying.

Today, I'm sober by the grace of God and my mom's prayer. During Lent, as we reflect on the paschal mystery, I think of my mother praying for me as she watched me suffer through the throes of my addiction. Who knows what Mary prayed for at the foot of the cross as she watched her son suffer? What I do know is that the story of my sixteen years of sobriety is a story of resurrection—and a testament to the power of prayer.

· grace ·

What Do Advent and Parenthood Have in Common?

Advent. 'Tis a time of waiting; of patience, but not passivity. Advent is mostly a time of preparation. Sounds a lot like parenthood, doesn't it?

We do what we can now, but we must wait until teenagers mature to see how our efforts pan out. We work to prepare them so that they'll be ready to handle the challenges they'll face in college and in adulthood. Even more importantly, we work to prepare them to enter God's kingdom.

While raising teenagers may sometimes feel more like Lent than Advent, the readings from the Advent season offer hope of God's promise. The prophet Isaiah proclaims that the glory and splendor of God will be revealed as the parched land of the desert blooms with abundant flowers, leading to rejoicing (Isaiah 35:1–2).

Saint James continues this theme by reminding us in his epistle how the farmer waits for the precious fruit of the earth, being patient with his crop until it receives the early and late rains: "You too must be patient. Make your hearts firm, because the coming of the Lord is at hand" (James 5:8).

We hope and pray that our efforts at loving and preparing teenagers will lead to the blossoming of their faith. But just as the Jews waited for the Messiah and we wait for Christ's second coming, we know we must be patient to realize the fruition of our efforts and the fulfillment of God's promise.

Jesus asks the followers of John the Baptist what they went out to see in the desert. His words question us why we do what we do. What are you waiting for? Why this preparation?

The answer comes in the form of the Good News: We want for us and for those we love to receive Christ's promise of everlasting life. Everything we do, as in Advent, is preparation toward the readiness of joining Christ in the kingdom.

We know God delivers. The blossoms will come—in the desert and in the kingdom. Christ will come. At Christmas and again. Our part is to be patient—but not passive. To be prepared.

· grace ·

Reach Out and Touch Someone

Hanging above my desk where I write is a detail from the famous scene Michelangelo painted on the Sistine Chapel. It depicts the moment of creation when God, hoisted by angels, reaches out to Adam, reclining on a rock. Actually, it is the moment just before Creation, right before God's extended finger reaches Adam's limp and lifeless hand. I have stared at the scene often while waiting for the inspiration to write, fearing that the creative spirit is frozen in time as God in the painting and that no life will ever spring from my keyboard.

The scene also suggests the relationship of an adult with a teenager. There the teenager reclines—in an easy chair watching television, in the corner of a classroom doodling, in the back seat of the car plugged into a Discman—and the adult strains to make a connection. Not that I mean to exalt the older person to God-like status—we're all equals, of course, in God's creation and eyes. But it seems if we make the effort to reach out, we can establish a connection and breathe life into that relationship.

It's the extra effort that sparks that life—taking your son or daughter fishing, going to his or her soccer game, asking questions about the subjects that interest them. In that moment, the connection might occur and your teenager may come to life.

Reminds me of a boy named Dan, a sullen kid who made it clear through his body language and facial expressions that he didn't like me and didn't want to have anything to do with me. He showed me all of the warmth of that rock Adam reclined upon. One day, when I found out he liked baseball, I asked him if he wanted to play catch. Surprise, he did. We tossed a baseball back and forth for about twenty minutes, and during that time we became buddies. Through the grace of the creative spirit, my effort of reaching out had brought new life to our relationship.

Not every effort has similar results, and often we have to strain longer and harder than I did that day, but it helps me to remember that scene of God reaching out to Adam. Even though it hasn't happened yet in that scene, we know how the story ends—or starts. We trust that God will bring new life through the effort of reaching out.

· grace ·

He Lives on in the Lives He Touched

On Easter Sunday morning, the sun broke free from a bank of clouds and sparkled on the lake. The symbolism seemed a bit heavy-handed, but I was willing to grant its author that indulgence, considering the occasion. Even when not as obvious, reminders of the Resurrection surround us.

Beyond the ice melting and the grass greening, there's evidence of new life in the recently retired man who finally feels rested and relaxed, in the child who proudly recites what she's learned that week in school, and in those catechumens receiving the sacrament of Baptism at the Easter Vigil. And, of course, as Jesus' story reminds us, there's resurrection in death.

Our memory of the deceased keeps them alive in our lives. During Lent, I find myself thinking often of a friend who died several years ago on Ash Wednesday.

Jon was a high school teacher and had a wonderful way with kids. Tall and gangly, he once told me he didn't wear shorts because he had such gnarly knees. His open and respectful manner inspired trust and respect from teenagers. His expectation of excellence often motivated students to work harder to deliver.

Ten years ago, we co-facilitated a support group of students struggling to stay sober. Of the many groups I've facilitated over the years, this one came together more closely than any other.

There were probably two reasons for the group's special cohesion. The first was the five students themselves. Committed to being honest, which is the prescription for recovery, they openly shared their feelings and challenged one another when they suspected they were holding something back. The second was Jon. He had a way of bringing out the honesty and goodness in the group. He was able to affirm those he met and steer the students to new levels of growth.

Jon died of cancer in his mid-forties without any children of his own, but I believe he lives on in the students whose lives he touched. I know I'm a different person for having known him. When I find myself emulating some of his practices, I feel his memory alive in me.

That's a moment of resurrection. After celebrating Christ's Resurrection on Easter, I wonder, how does He live on in us?

· *grace* ·

Examining Our Desert Experiences

A local church asked me to speak to its Confirmation class about the Lenten theme of temptation. We started with the Gospel story that kicked off Lent: Jesus' temptation in the desert. That story and theirs reinforced the power of telling our stories of temptation if we are to live out our faith.

When I asked the group of ninth and tenth graders and their sponsors to reflect on times they had been tempted, then to discuss them, they had some difficulty with the exercise. Some said it was hard to pinpoint specific temptations; others that it was uncomfortable discussing them. Not surprising because temptation can lead us to act in ways we later wish we hadn't.

Yet, identifying our temptations is the first step in facing them. For instance, anger is a source of temptation to act or say something we know we'll later regret. When we get angry, we need to do something to avoid that temptation, say talk to a friend, exercise, or write in a journal to calm down.

Hearing others tell their story of facing the same temptation can take the shame out of our own experience by simply reflecting our humanity. In the desert, after fasting for forty days and forty nights, Jesus was tempted to turn stones into bread, and was vulnerable to His hunger, that is, His humanity. Just like us, Jesus faced temptation.

Yet, Jesus stayed true to himself and resisted the temptation by relying on His faith. So I had the group write about and discuss a time when they had done the same. One boy had found a wallet with money in it but turned it in. He did not receive a monetary reward, but he did receive one worth more than any dollar amount—integrity.

This reward is too often overlooked. We give ourselves a hard time when we screw up, but when we do the right thing, we often do not pay as much internal attention. These are little victories of faith that I believe deserve to be celebrated, especially in our prayer. Doing so can help us stay true to our faith the next time we face temptation.

Knowing that we are not alone in the temptations we face and remembering the victories we've had resisting them in the past can strengthen our faith. Talking about them with teenagers will do the same.

· grace ·

Love Is in the Air

After a dismal performance at his tennis match, Tommy apologized to me, his coach. The girl he had asked to a formal dance had said no.

The next day, he played wonderfully in practice—the girl had reconsidered and said yes. Ah, spring.

Love is in the air. The fish spawn, the frogs mate, the ducklings hatch. And the earth is busy, too: The grass greens, leaves sprout and take shape, tulips push forth, and fruit trees blossom. The darkened landscape takes on the vibrant activity, colors, and fragrance of creation.

The mystery of the Resurrection is present throughout, transforming darkness into light, death into new life.

Love has the power to transform more than one's tennis game; it transforms one's life. Love carries the creative power of the Resurrection, creating new life in those it touches.

I know what Tommy was experiencing; loss and love have touched my life. Several years ago, in the wake of a breakup, I doubted that I would ever love again. The grief felt permanent. The landscape of my love life looked as bleak and barren as any Minnesota field in November.

But spring arrived. Maria walked into my life, and I fell in love again. Two years later we married—in the spring. While I won't indulge in the story of our romance, suffice it to say that our relationship has been happier than I imagined one could ever be.

I am amazed that I was able to love again. But then, I am amazed every year when the trees bloom after the long winter. And when I hear the Resurrection story on Easter after the Passion and death of Jesus.

I suppose I shouldn't be so amazed. I see what love does in young people's lives; I see spring happen each year. Yet, feeling God's presence this close and this active in my own life when I had all but given up astounds me.

When Maria expresses her love for me, I experience the miracle of resurrection, over and over again. Yes, God lives, and God loves. And we live again.

· grace ·

Resurrection—Wherever Life Rises

The days grow longer, the birds return, the earth thaws. It's Easter time, season of the Resurrection.

I love this time of year—reliving Christ's suffering through the Stations of the Cross, hearing the Passion narration during Holy Week, participating in the story of the Eucharist on Holy Thursday, and, of course, rejoicing in the story of Christ rising from the dead Easter morning. The story of Christ's Resurrection, his triumph over sin, forms the basis of our faith.

Our belief in the paschal mystery reveals stories of life triumphing over death in many ways all around us.

There is resurrection in the student in one of my classes who failed second quarter but worked extra hard the next quarter to pull off a B; in the student who got cut from the tennis team one year but came out the next year and made it; in the student, painfully shy as a sophomore, who, as a senior, played his guitar publicly and performed the lead role in class projects. That's life rising from defeat.

There's resurrection in the apology I needed to make to a colleague who forgave me with a hug; in the apology from another colleague only five minutes after the fact; and in the mutual apology I made to and received from a student, necessary on both sides after we lost our tempers. That's life rising over resentment.

There's resurrection in the sixty-seven-year-old woman completing her bachelor's degree; in the retired hockey star playing another professional game on his sixty-ninth birthday; and in the seventy-eight-year-old political leader who refuses taking revenge in his crusade to lead a country torn by apartheid to reconciliation (all stories I read one Easter week). That's life rising over age.

Everywhere I look, it seems, there's life rising. Sure, I see the pain and despair as well, but it's there where resurrection begins. Sometimes, telling the stories of life triumphing can give us the faith and hope to sustain us, or another, to the next resurrection.

Conclusion

Grace waits. It's at work in your life, waiting for you to notice.

I hope that you, after reading these anecdotes and observations from my life, can find the similar moments in your own when Christ becomes present. Grace happens, that's for sure. The trick is to become aware of it.

Becoming aware of it in our interactions with teenagers may have seemed unlikely at the onset, but by now I trust that you believe it's possible. Recognizing grace requires an openness of mind and spirit, a willingness to set aside preconceived notions so that we may encounter Christ however he presents himself to us. You have to buy into the belief that Christ is indeed present in everyone we meet, teenagers not excluded.

Certain attitudes seem to help us notice grace at work—gratitude, service, and compassion. They open us up to Christ's presence.

Certainly, when we're on the lookout for grace, we're more likely to spot it. Writing about grace has worked for me. I find myself more likely to approach a situation looking for the goodness to be discovered in it. You might try the same with a journal.

Another method I'm fond of is a variation of the Ignatian examination of conscience. At the end of the day—or any point in the day when you can find time—review the past twenty-four hours. Ask, Where was grace at work in my life? When did I sense Christ's presence? You might wish to record your observations guided by these questions in a journal as well.

A Jesuit priest offered me two simple prayers that I'll pass along, two prayers that he says every day that help put him in touch with God active in his life. In the morning, upon waking, he says, "Surprise me." At night, when he goes to bed, he says, "Thanks." That works.

My prayer for you is that your life be as abundantly blessed as mine has been by the teenagers I've known. May your faith let you see the face of God in them.

Acknowledgments *(continued from copyright page)*

All scriptural quotations are from the New American Bible with Revised New Testament and Revised Psalms. Copyright © 1991, 1986, and 1970 by the Confraternity of Christian Doctrine, Washington, DC. Used by permission of the copyright owner. All rights reserved. No part of the New American Bible may be reproduced in any form without permission in writing from the copyright owner.

The summary on jokes on page 15 is from *Voices and Their Relation to the Unconscious,* by Sigmund Freud (New York: W. W. Norton & Co., 1963), page 103. Copyright © 1963 by W. W. Norton & Co.

The quotation on page 29 is from *Letters to a Young Poet,* by Rainer Maria Rilke, translated by Stephen Mitchell (New York: Vintage Books, 1984), pages 34–35. Copyright © 1984 by Stephen Mitchell.

The poem on page 40 is from "Aurora Leigh," by Elizabeth Barrett Browning, in *The Oxford Book of English Mystical Verse,* edited by D. H. S. Nicholson and A. H. E. Lee (Oxford: The Clarendon Press, 1917). Information accessed March 26, 2002, at *www.bartleby.com/236/86.html*.

The quotation on page 46 is from "Virginia, There Is a Santa Claus," by Francis Pharcellus Church, in the *New York Sun* (1897). Information accessed March 27, 2002, at *www.educa.rcanaria.es/usr/zonzamas/virginia.htm*.

The quotation on page 53 is from "The Force That Through the Green Fuse Drives the Flower," by Dylan Thomas, in *Chief Modern Poets of Britain and America,* vol. 1, edited by Gerald D. Sanders, John H. Nelson, and M. L. Rosenthal (New York: Macmillan Publishing, Co., Inc., 1970), page I-395. Copyright © 1970 by Macmillan Publishing Co., Inc.

The quotation on page 58 is from "The Gift Outright," by Robert Frost (poem read at the Kennedy Inauguration, 1961). Information accessed March 26, 2002, at *www.americaslibrary.gov/pages/jb_0120_frost_3.html*.

The prayer on page 60 is by Brother Roger of Taizé, © Ateliers et Presses de Taizé, 71250 Taizé Community, France. Used with permission of Taizé.

The quotation from the Sister Hazel liner notes on page 70 is from the album *Somewhere More Familiar* by Sister Hazel (Crooked Chimney Music, Inc., 1996). Copyright © 1996 by Crooked Chimney Music, Inc.

The quotation on page 79 is from *Anna Karenina,* by Leo Tolstoy, translated by Joel Carmichael (Bantam Books, Inc., 1960), page 428. Copyright © 1960 by Bantam Books, Inc. Used with permission of Bantam Books, Inc.

The quotation on page 87 is from "The Servant Song," by Richard Gillard, in *Scripture in Song.* Copyright © 1977 Scripture in Song (a division of Integrity Music, Inc.)/ASCAP c/o Integrity Music, Inc., 1000 Cody Road, Mobile, AL 36695. The song was accessed March 26, 2002, at *www.xsite.net/~videoc/Jon/JB.html.* Used with permission of Integrity Music, Inc.

The poem on page 101 is from "Coming or Going," by Robert Bly Dogen, in *The Soul Is Here for Its Own Joy: Sacred Poems from Many Cultures,* edited by Robert Bly Dogen (Hopewell, NJ: The Ecco Press, 1995), page 210. Copyright © 1995 by Robert Bly Dogen.